AS-Level
Critical Thinking

This book contains everything you need to know for AS-Level Critical Thinking
— without any unnecessary waffle.

It'll take you step by step through the kinds of questions you'll get in the actual
exams and give you lots of hints and tips to stop you missing out on vital marks.

There are loads of warm-up and exam-style questions so you can prepare for the big day
as well as a CD-ROM with multiple choice tests just like the one you'll get in the Unit 2 exam.

And of course, we've done our best to make the whole thing vaguely entertaining for you.

Complete Revision and Practice

Exam Board: OCR

Published by CGP

Editors:
Josephine Gibbons, Rachael Powers, Rebecca Tate

Contributors:
Peter Callaghan

Proofreaders:
Andy Park, Kevin Smith

CD-ROM produced by Chris Dennett

ISBN: 978 1 84762 599 1

Groovy Website: www.cgpbooks.co.uk
Jolly bits of clipart from CorelDRAW®

Printed by Elanders Ltd, Newcastle upon Tyne.

Based on the classic CGP style created by Richard Parsons.

Contents

How the Exams Work

Welcome to AS-level Critical Thinking — a guide to how to bamboozle your friends with bewildering logic, convincingly argue that left is right, hone your mind into a razor sharp tool of witty debate... and, last but not least, pass your AS exam. These two pages contain really useful information on what to expect in the exam and the types of questions you'll see.

AS *Critical Thinking* is divided into *Two Units*

1) Each unit is **assessed** by an **exam** lasting **1½ hours**.
2) Both units are worth the **same** number of **marks**.
3) For the **Unit 1** exam you'll need to learn the information in **Sections 1 and 2** of this book. You **won't** need to know **anything** from **Sections 3 to 5**.
4) The **Unit 2** exam tests the material covered in **Sections 3 to 5** of this book, as well as lots of the terms that were explained in **Section 1**.

Jim quickly discovered that he did his best critical thinking in the nude.

In the *Unit One* exam there are *Two Sections*

1) Here's a rough **guide** to how to use your **time** in the **Unit 1** exam.
2) Don't worry if you can't remember all this information on the day of the exam — it'll be on the **front** of the **exam paper** to remind you.

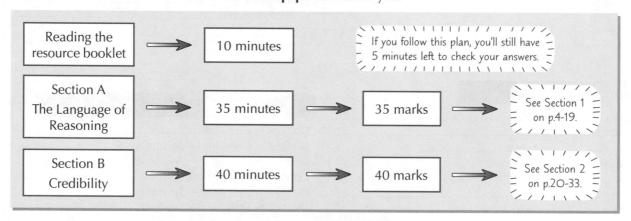

Reading the resource booklet	10 minutes		*If you follow this plan, you'll still have 5 minutes left to check your answers.*
Section A — The Language of Reasoning	35 minutes	35 marks	*See Section 1 on p.4-19.*
Section B — Credibility	40 minutes	40 marks	*See Section 2 on p.20-33.*

In the *Unit Two* exam there are *Three Sections*

On the **Unit 2** exam paper, you **won't** be given as much **advice** on how to use your **time**. Here's a **suggestion** though:

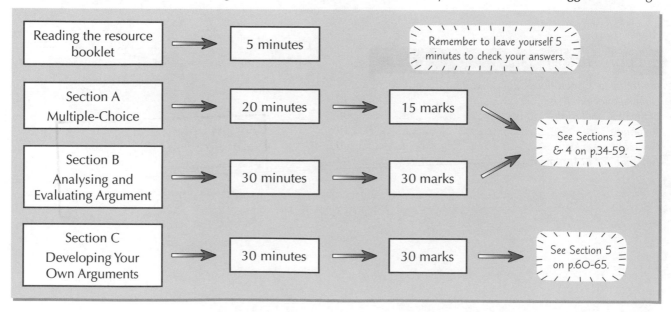

Reading the resource booklet	5 minutes		*Remember to leave yourself 5 minutes to check your answers.*
Section A — Multiple-Choice	20 minutes	15 marks	*See Sections 3 & 4 on p.34-59.*
Section B — Analysing and Evaluating Argument	30 minutes	30 marks	
Section C — Developing Your Own Arguments	30 minutes	30 marks	*See Section 5 on p.60-65.*

What You'll Be Marked On

Library

You'll be tested on *Three Assessment Objectives (AOs)*

1) AS Critical Thinking tests **three** different **assessment objectives** which we've **explained** below. Both Unit 1 and Unit 2 test **all** three objectives.

2) The examiner will also be **marking** you on your **spelling** and **grammar** in the longer answers.

AO1 — *Analyse* Argument

1) **Analysing** an argument means **identifying** the different **elements** it contains, e.g. reasons, conclusion etc.

2) **Questions** testing AO1 often **start** with the words, 'Identify...', 'Name...' or 'State...'

3) The examiner says you've got to use **technical** terms '**appropriately** and **precisely**'. This means you'll have to know the proper **names** for all the different argument **elements**.

4) If you're asked to 'state' an argument element, you'll have to **quote directly** from the document.

5) Here's an **example** of the **type** of question that tests **AO1**:

> State the main conclusion of the argument found in Document 1.

AO2 — *Evaluate* Argument

1) **Evaluating** an argument means deciding how **effective** it is — whether it manages to **convince** us that its **conclusion** is true.

2) You might have to do this by looking at how **well** reasons **support** the conclusion, looking for any **problems** with the argument (**flaws**) or deciding how **credible** (believable) the **sources** in an argument are.

3) **Questions** testing AO2 often **start** with words like, 'Evaluate...', 'Explain...' or 'Assess...'

4) Here's an **example** of the **type** of question that tests **AO2**:

> Consider the argument in Document 2. Evaluate how far the reasons given support its conclusion.

AO3 — *Develop* your own Argument

1) **Developing** arguments involves coming up with your **own** arguments (or argument **elements**).

2) **Section C** of the Unit 2 exam is **all** about developing your own, **longer** arguments, but there are also questions in Unit 1 and the **other** sections of Unit 2 where you'll be tested on AO3.

3) **Questions** testing AO3 **often** start like this: '**Suggest** one more reason...', '**Give** an alternative explanation...', '**Write** your own argument...'

4) According to the **examiner**, your arguments need to be written '**clearly** and **accurately** in a **concise** and **logical** manner'. This means no **waffling**, and using **exact** quotes when you need to. It's also a good idea to **plan** longer answers.

5) Here's an **example** of the **type** of question that tests **AO3**:

> Suggest one more reason why teaching children via videolink over the internet is a bad idea.

You knit one — and then you knit two...

Not the most exciting start, I admit, but the good thing is you don't have to learn what's on these two pages. It may seem a bit early to be thinking about the exam, but it's really important that you know what's coming. Make sure you know roughly how long to spend on each section of the exam, and which bits of this book you'll need to learn for each unit.

Arguments, Reasons & Conclusions

Now we've got all that dull exam stuff out of the way, it's time to get started on the real Critical Thinking — hurrah.

What is an **Argument**?

1) In Critical Thinking, an **argument** is a piece of writing or a speech that tries to persuade you to accept something.

2) The thing that the argument is trying to persuade you to accept is called the argument's **conclusion** — it could be a suggestion, an idea, a belief or a theory.

3) The conclusion is backed up by **reasons** — these are the parts of the argument that aim to persuade you to accept the conclusion.

4) A **statement** that **isn't** backed up by any **reasons** isn't an argument or a conclusion — it's an **assertion**.

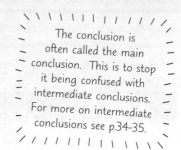
The conclusion is often called the main conclusion. This is to stop it being confused with intermediate conclusions. For more on intermediate conclusions see p.34-35.

An argument must have **Only One** conclusion and **At Least One** reason

Remember — an argument has **at least one** reason and **only one** conclusion. If it doesn't then it's **not** an argument. Here are some examples of basic arguments:

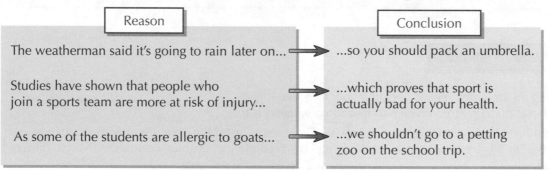

Reason	Conclusion
The weatherman said it's going to rain later on...	...so you should pack an umbrella.
Studies have shown that people who join a sports team are more at risk of injury...	...which proves that sport is actually bad for your health.
As some of the students are allergic to goats...	...we shouldn't go to a petting zoo on the school trip.

A difference of opinion is **Not** an **Argument**

The example below **isn't** an **argument** because it doesn't contain any **reasons**.

There's no reason backing this up — so it's an assertion.

Custard creams are the best biscuits ever.

Yuck! Pink wafers are much better.

No they're NOT.

Yes they ARE!

Scuffle, argy bargy, fisticuffs, ... but not an argument.

Common Notation helps show argument **Structures** clearly

1) The **structure** of an argument is all its **different parts**, such as the conclusion and the reasons, and the **logical way** that they're **linked** to each other.

2) There are **many ways** to structure an argument — it doesn't always just go Reason ⟶ Conclusion.

3) A quick way to show the structure of an argument is to use **common notation**. Common notation **replaces** important **words** in Critical Thinking with **letters**. Reason is shortened to 'R' and conclusion is shortened to 'C'. The common notation for an argument with one reason and one conclusion is: R ⟶ C.

4) If there's **more than one** reason in an argument then they're **numbered**, like this: **R1, R2** etc.

Arguments, Reasons & Conclusions

Changing the **Order** doesn't change the **Argument's Structure**

You can change the order of an argument's parts without changing the **logical link** between the **conclusion** and the **reasons**:

You should pack an umbrella because the weatherman said it's going to rain later on.

The weatherman said it's going to rain later on. You're going to be outside all day, and you don't want to ruin your hairdo. You should pack an umbrella.

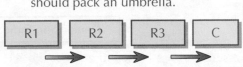

The weatherman said it's going to rain later on. You should pack an umbrella. You're going to be outside all day, and you don't want to ruin your hairdo.

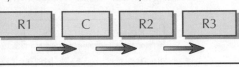

This means you **can't tell** if something is a reason or a conclusion from where it's placed — the conclusion isn't always at the end. Instead, look at the **meaning** of each sentence and work out if the writer is concluding or reasoning.

Quote your way to **Exam Success**

In the exam, you'll probably be asked to "**state** the reasons" or "**state** the main conclusion" of an argument. It's important to **quote directly** from the text and to write out the **whole conclusion**. For example:

Q1 Read the text below and state the main conclusion of the argument.

Companies spend millions of pounds on TV advertising. But most people just channel-hop instead of paying attention in the advert break. Online advertising, however, places banners on websites used by the company's target market — so it's guaranteed to reach the right people. Also, online ads contain links to the product: they're interactive and instant which makes them more attention-grabbing. Therefore, companies should stop wasting money on TV adverts, and invest in online advertising instead.

1) This is the **main conclusion** of the argument: ➡️ "companies should stop wasting money on TV adverts, and invest in online advertising instead". ✓

2) When you write your answer, **don't** use an **ellipsis** (...) — you might **leave out** an important part of the conclusion.

"companies should... invest in online advertising" ✗

E.g. this answer gives **part** of the **conclusion** — that companies should **invest** in **online advertising**. But it **misses out** the **part** about how money spent on **television ads** would be **better spent** on online ones.

3) Don't **rephrase** the conclusion, either. ➡️ It's silly to spend money on TV adverts — online ads are much better. ✗

Practice Questions

Q1 Complete this sentence: "The reasons in an argument are the parts _____"
   a) at the beginning.   b) that the writer wants you to accept.   c) that explain why you should accept the conclusion.

Q2 What's wrong with this answer: 'The argument's main conclusion is "you should pack... your scarf"' ?

Exam Question

Q1 State the main conclusion of the argument presented in the passage below.   [3 marks]

   "The cakes and biscuits are not selling very well. Fruit snacks will be more popular because many customers are on diets. Therefore we should start making fruit salads and smoothies. They're cheaper too, so there's no reason not to."

So remember, never ever use ellipses...

That first plunge into the clear waters of Critical Thinking should've awakened your senses and invigorated your mind. Or maybe you're just disappointed that the definition of an argument didn't involve a bit more violence. I wanted drama, I wanted passion, I wanted... at least a kick in the ankles or glass of water in the face. All I got was "one reason and one conclusion". Sigh...

Argument Indicators

These pages are all about argument indicators — nifty little words that make spotting conclusions and reasons a bit easier. But be careful, they might also lead you down the garden path and onto a wild goose chase...

Argument Indicators help Identify different parts of the argument

1) With some arguments, it's not **immediately clear** which bits are the reasons and which bit is the conclusion.

2) **Argument indicators** are **words** that writers **often** use to show that a reason or conclusion is coming up.

3) Looking out for these words in the text can help you spot the **different parts** of the argument.

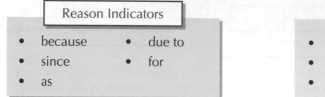

Reason Indicators	
• because	• due to
• since	• for
• as	

Conclusion Indicators	
• therefore	• consequently
• thus	• should
• so	• which is why

4) Here are some **examples**. The **reason indicators** are highlighted in **blue** and the **conclusion indicators** are in **orange**:

> Even though it's raining, you <u>shouldn't</u> take your umbrella. <u>Since</u> it's blowing a gale force wind, it'll just break as soon as you walk out the door, especially <u>because</u> it's a cheap, flimsy one.

> We <u>should</u> go on a nice long walk, <u>because</u> we haven't had much exercise recently and <u>as</u> it's such a beautiful day.

> It's really important to have good posture when you're sitting down. <u>Therefore</u>, you <u>should</u> make sure your chair is at the correct height and angle, <u>because</u> if you're too low or high it makes you slouch.

5) You might get a question in the exam asking you to state the indicator words that have been used in a passage of text.

Argument indicators Don't Always work

Argument indicators can be useful, but it's important to remember that they are **only a guideline**. **Don't assume** something is a reason or a conclusion **just because** it begins with a reason or conclusion indicator.

1) Some arguments don't contain **any** indicator words at all:

> It's a poorly made product, there's no reliable research into market demand, and their projected sales targets are unrealistic. I don't recommend investing in their company.

No helpful hints here...

When her indicators stopped working, Kate found other ways to get attention.

2) Argument indicators can be used in **other contexts** as well:

> We **should** consider both sides of the debate before criticising beauty contests. It's easy to condemn something that seems **so** focused on the superficial, but perhaps they do promote something other than shallowness. For example, many contestants argue that the contests encourage public speaking and **therefore** improve their self-confidence.

This is the conclusion...

...but you could be misled by these words which look like conclusion indicators.

Argument Indicators

Use the 'Therefore Test' to check you're Correct

Argument indicators can point you in the **right direction**, but if you're still unsure
that you've found the conclusion, you can double-check using the **'Therefore Test'**:

1) Put the word 'therefore' in front of a statement to see if it **works** as a **conclusion**.

2) Then insert the word 'because' in front of the other statements
   to check the conclusion **follows** from them as **reasons**.

3) If it makes sense, then you have **correctly identified** the different parts of the argument.

4) The 'Therefore Test' is also helpful if you think there are **misleading** argument indicators
   in the text, or **none** at all. For example, it would be useful to check the previous argument:

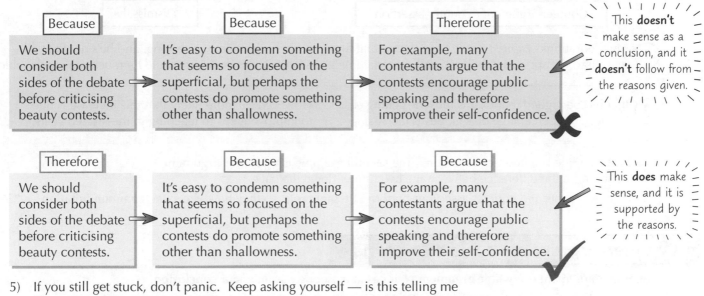

5) If you still get stuck, don't panic. Keep asking yourself — is this telling me
   why I should accept something... or is it telling me **what** I should accept?

Practice Questions

Q1   a)   Find all the argument indicators used in the argument below.
       b)   Use the "therefore test" to identify the conclusion.
       c)   Which word does not indicate a conclusion in this passage, even though it can be used as a conclusion indicator?

> "History isn't an appropriate subject for schools because History lessons are affected by the preconceptions
> of those who set and teach the syllabus. The lessons will be biased since, even if there aren't any obvious
> distortions of fact, historical events that support current social ideals will be highlighted and therefore other
> historical events will be neglected. It is dangerous to expose children to such tainted information."

Exam Question

Q1   State three argument indicator words used in the paragraph below.   [3 marks]

> "Too much money is spent on space exploration, especially since countries suffering from famine and disease could do
> so much good with that money. A world free from disease, a world where no-one lives in hunger, would be a truly great
> achievement. Deciding that Pluto is not a planet after all is nowhere near as impressive. Therefore, instead of spending a lot
> of money, time and effort on vain projects such as the space programme, we should address the problems we face on Earth."

Sighs, tuts, angry glares — some argument indicators are clearer than others...

Phew — there's a lot of trial and error when it comes to identifying reasons and conclusions in more complicated arguments.
Luckily there's lots of things you can do to get totally awesome at it. Like reading newspaper articles and deciding what the
conclusion is, or listening out for reasons to buy stuff on adverts. Hurrah for watching the telly and pretending it's revision...

Counter-Arguments & Counter-Assertions

Reasons — check. Conclusions — check. There's not much to this arguing malarky is there... Oh, apart from all the other things in this section that you'll need to learn, starting with counter-arguments and counter-assertions...

Counter-Assertions and Counter-Arguments disagree with the Main Conclusion

1) Some arguments include **counter-arguments** or **counter-assertions**. **Counter-assertions** and **counter-arguments** are parts of the argument which **oppose** the main **conclusion**.

2) Showing why the counter-argument or counter-assertion is **wrong** can **strengthen** an argument's conclusion. Showing a counter-argument is wrong is called **dismissing** a counter-argument.

3) Another reason for including counter-arguments in an argument is to make it seem **balanced** and **well thought through**.

Counter-argument / counter-assertion	Dismissal
① My friend thinks *Light-Hearted Love Romp*, that film with Brad DiPaprio in it, will be really entertaining...	...but his last film was boring, and he's not fit at all. *Moody Vampire Angst* would be much more enjoyable.
② It could be argued that exams must be getting easier because the percentage of A grades is increasing.	However, it's more likely that this increase is due to improvements in teaching in the last ten years.

4) The **first** example is a **counter-assertion**. The **second** example is a **counter-argument**. There's more on the difference between the two further down the page.

5) Counter-arguments and counter-assertions perform the same **role**, so they have the same **common notation** — '**CA**'.

Counter-Arguments contain Reasons

1) A counter argument is a **whole argument** — it has at least one **reason** and a **conclusion**.

2) A **counter-assertion** is just a **statement** without any supporting reasons.

Counter-argument

A counter-argument has reasons... ...to support the conclusion... ...that is then dismissed.

Some people think that because social networking sites encourage you to post your date of birth and contact details in a public space, the Internet makes people's private lives and important data too easily accessible. This actually isn't a problem at all, because there are all sorts of security settings to protect your information.

Counter-assertion

A counter-assertion has an unsupported assertion... ...that is then dismissed.

Some people think the Internet makes people's private lives and important data too easily accessible. This actually isn't a problem at all, because there are all sorts of security settings to protect your information.

Look out for Reasons that Don't Support the author's Conclusion

1) The **exam** might ask a **question** like this:

> Q1 State the counter-argument used in the argument below.

2) First, make sure you know the **conclusion** of the **argument**. Then, look for reasons that **go against** the **conclusion** — these are almost always part of a **counter-argument**.

3) It's also worth looking out for these **words**:

- Despite this
- However
- Although
- It has been claimed
- Contrary to this
- Some people argue

4) Be careful though — most of these words can indicate the main conclusion **or** a counter-argument. They're just a rough guideline — you'll still have to pay attention to the **meaning** of the sentences.

Simple Hypothetical Reasoning

Hypothetical reasoning is all about what could happen if something else did happen. It contains a lot of "ifs", and you know what they say — if "ifs and buts" were candies 'n' nuts, we'd all love critical thinking.

Hypothetical Reasoning is in the Form — "If this..., Then that..."

1) Sometimes an argument will make a claim that **predicts** what **might happen** as a **result** of something else. This is called **hypothetical reasoning**.

2) It's usually in the form "**If this** happens, **then that** will happen". For example — "**If** you buy a pet llama, **then** you will never run out of wool".

3) But the '**then**' is not always stated, e.g. "If the door opens, the llamas will escape".

4) Sometimes the "**if**" is not stated, e.g. "Supposing you opened the door, then the llamas would escape".

5) Or the **order** might be **reversed**, e.g. "The llamas will run wild and free with the wind in their wool and the world at their feet, if I open the door".

6) **Hypothetical reasoning** can be used as a **reason** or **conclusion** in an argument. For example:

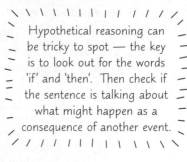
Hypothetical reasoning can be tricky to spot — the key is to look out for the words 'if' and 'then'. Then check if the sentence is talking about what might happen as a consequence of another event.

Here, the hypothetical reasoning is a reason.

> If bargain stores keep demanding cheap labour, **then** developing countries will never improve their dangerous factory conditions. Therefore, we should stop buying products from bargain stores.

> My school has a strict dress code and the teachers always punish us if we don't follow it. So **if** I wear too much jewellery to school, **then** it will be confiscated.

Here, the hypothetical reasoning is the conclusion.

It's Important to Explain Why something is Hypothetical

1) In the **exam**, you might be asked to **explain why** something is **hypothetical**:

> Q1   Find an example of hypothetical reasoning used in argument A and explain your answer.

2) This might seem a bit **daft** but you **can't** say "This is my answer because it's an example of hypothetical reasoning, which is what you asked for".

3) Instead, **explain** what's going on in your example that **makes** it **hypothetical**: ➡️

> This is hypothetical reasoning because the conclusion refers to a consequence (the jewellery "will be confiscated") that depends upon a conditional event (wearing "too much jewellery to school") in order to happen.

Practice Questions

Q1   What is the difference between counter-arguments and counter-assertions?

Q2   Which of the following usually indicates a counter-argument?
a) "consequently"   b) a conclusion without any reasons   c) reasons that disagree with the main conclusion

Exam Question

Q1   Identify the hypothetical reasoning in the paragraph below and explain your answer.   [4 marks]

"The future will be a terrible place. Global warming will increase extreme weather conditions, countries will disappear under rising sea levels, and many species will become extinct. Our grandchildren's children will be the ones who suffer if we keep polluting the environment."

It could be argued that this was the most exciting page ever...

However, you might just be glad it's over. Either way, at least arguments are looking a bit more lively now. Imagine if it was nothing but reasons and conclusion, reasons and conclusion. Easy, yes — but very very dull. But now, with a pinch of counter-arguments and a sprinkling of hypothetical seasoning (ahem... reasoning) you've stewed yourself a very tasty argument indeed.

Assumptions

This is a tricky bit. Assumptions are about looking for things that aren't written in the text, or "reading between the lines"...

An **Assumption** is an **Unstated Reason** that is **Needed** for the argument to work

1) In Critical Thinking, an **assumption** is an unstated **reason** which is **needed** for the argument to **make sense**.

2) An assumption must be **necessary** to the conclusion. It is needed to **connect** the **reasons** to the **conclusion**. Without it, the argument **wouldn't work**.

3) An argument can have **more than one** assumption.

4) Just because an argument relies upon assumptions, that doesn't mean it's **weak**. **Most** arguments **rely** on some sort of assumption, as we can see if we look at some arguments from earlier in the book:

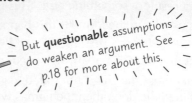

But **questionable** assumptions do weaken an argument. See p.18 for more about this.

Argument		Assumption
The weatherman said it's going to rain later on, so you should pack an umbrella.	→	You will want to protect yourself from the rain, and an umbrella is the best way to do that.
As some of the students are allergic to goats, we shouldn't go to a petting zoo on the school trip.	→	The petting zoo will aggravate the students' allergies because it has goats.

Find **Assumptions** by looking for **Missing Steps** in the **Argument**

1) First, **identify** the argument's **reasons** and **conclusion**.

2) Then think about how the two are **connected** — what are the **missing steps** that join the reasons to the conclusion?

Here's an **Example**

R1 It is the police's duty to protect the public from danger.

R2 High-speed chases are the only way to catch some criminals.

C Therefore, high-speed chases are needed so police can do their duty.

This argument makes an **assumption** about the need for high-speed chases. It claims that high-speed chases are a way of catching criminals, and the police need to protect the public from danger. To get from these reasons to **needing** high-speed chases, the author **must assume** this:

Assumption
A significant proportion of criminals are more dangerous to the public than high-speed chases.

Saying "a significant proportion of criminals" instead of "all criminals" makes sure the assumption isn't too strong. See p.11 for more on this.

Another **Lovely** example

R1 Students need to be studying literature that improves their grasp of today's language.

R2 The language in Shakespeare's plays is centuries old, and students are often unable to understand the basic meaning, let alone the subtle wordplay and imagery.

C Therefore, Shakespeare should be dropped from the syllabus in favour of more modern texts.

In this example, an **assumption** is made about the need to teach Shakespeare. The argument claims that students need to improve their English, and modern literature is better for doing this than Shakespeare. To get from these reasons to **dropping** Shakespeare from the syllabus the author **must assume** two things:

Assumption
Shakespeare has no other educational benefits.

+

Assumption
There is not room on the syllabus for both modern texts and Shakespeare.

Assumptions

Be **Precise** when **Formulating** assumptions

It's important to be very careful when answering questions about what an author is **assuming**. To get full marks you need to be as **clear** and **precise** as possible. Learn these **common mistakes** so you know to avoid them:

1) This is **too strong**: All criminals are more dangerous than high-speed chases. ✗

2) This is **too weak**: A few criminals might be more dangerous than high-speed chases. ✗

3) This isn't **relevant**: The police enjoy high-speed chases. ✗

It can be tricky to get the strength of the assumption correct. If an assumption doesn't seem realistic, there's a good chance it's too strong. If it seems too vague to support the conclusion, it's probably too weak. Phrases like "a significant proportion", "many" or "a large number" will help you to word an assumption so it's neither too strong, nor too weak.

Use the **Opposite Test** to check any **Assumptions** are **Correct**

Check that the assumptions you've found are **necessary** to the argument by inserting the **opposite** of the assumptions and seeing if the argument still works. This is called the **Opposite Test** (or Negative or Reverse Test). It works like this:

State the **reasons**:

This is one of the examples from p.10 — have a quick look to remind yourself of the assumptions found in the argument.

Students need to be studying literature that improves their grasp of today's language. The language in Shakespeare's plays is centuries old, and students are often unable to understand the basic meaning, let alone the subtle wordplay and imagery.

Insert the **exact opposite** of the assumptions you've identified:

Shakespeare **has** other educational benefits.

There **is** room on the syllabus for both modern texts and Shakespeare.

The conclusion doesn't make sense now — which proves that the author has to make the assumption for the argument to work.

Then see if the **conclusion** still **follows** from the **reasons**:

Therefore, Shakespeare should be dropped from the syllabus in favour of more modern texts.

Practice Questions

Q1 What is an assumption?
a) a necessary, written reason   b) a conclusion that is necessary but unstated   c) an unstated, necessary reason

Q2 An argument is thought to contain the assumption "boys are noisier than girls".
Which of the following should you use in the Opposite Test?
a) boys are not noisier than girls   b) boys are quieter than girls   c) girls are noisier than boys

Exam Question

Q1 State one assumption that is necessary to support the conclusion about parenting in the argument below. [3 marks]

"Marriage is the best atmosphere to raise a child, because each parent has another responsible, caring adult they can rely on to support them in difficult times. Also, one person cannot provide everything needed to raise a well-rounded individual. A husband and wife, as a team, will each contribute different but valuable life skills to the child."

Hee Haw. When you assume, you make a donkey out of u and me...

I think I quoted that incorrectly. But it doesn't matter, it's wrong anyway. Most arguments contain some kind of assumption. So whoever said that assumptions were always bad clearly didn't know what they were chatting about. You need to get the hang of finding assumptions, and there's only one way to do it — practise, practise, practise. Assuming you want to pass the exam...

SECTION ONE — THE LANGUAGE OF REASONING

Evidence & Examples

Examples and Evidence — no, it's not the tantalising new thriller from Dan Brown, it's yet more techniques that help to make arguments nice and persuasive. Read on, and prepare to be amazed...

Evidence is used to Support Reasons

1) Some arguments include **evidence**, e.g.
   - Results from studies presented as proportions, percentages, or graphs.
   - Quotes that give evidence of professional opinions.
2) The **purpose** of evidence is to **support** one of the argument's reasons.
3) Evidence makes the reasons more **convincing** — and more convincing reasons usually mean a better argument, e.g.

> You should eat more vegetables because they're good for you. Courgettes help prevent heart disease and carrots fight against premature ageing.

> It's important for young children to have a male role model. Research has revealed that 44% of people felt that having a male primary school teacher helped build their confidence. Therefore, we should encourage male graduates to become teachers.

Evidence can come from Research

1) Different types of **research** are often used as **evidence**.
2) This type of evidence **supports** reasons by providing **proof** that they're **true**.
3) Research usually falls into one of these **categories**:

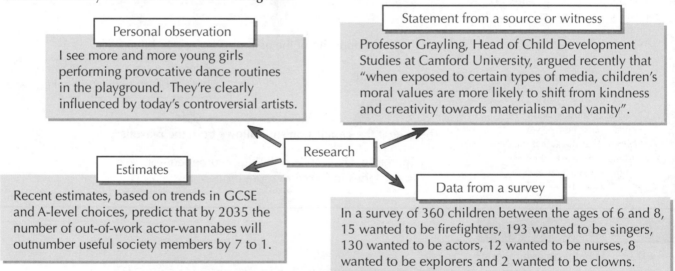

Personal observation

> I see more and more young girls performing provocative dance routines in the playground. They're clearly influenced by today's controversial artists.

Statement from a source or witness

> Professor Grayling, Head of Child Development Studies at Camford University, argued recently that "when exposed to certain types of media, children's moral values are more likely to shift from kindness and creativity towards materialism and vanity".

Estimates

> Recent estimates, based on trends in GCSE and A-level choices, predict that by 2035 the number of out-of-work actor-wannabes will outnumber useful society members by 7 to 1.

Data from a survey

> In a survey of 360 children between the ages of 6 and 8, 15 wanted to be firefighters, 193 wanted to be singers, 130 wanted to be actors, 12 wanted to be nurses, 8 wanted to be explorers and 2 wanted to be clowns.

Evidence can be presented as Statistics

1) When numbers are turned into percentages, proportions, graphs or charts they're known as **statistics**.
2) Arguments use statistics because they're **easier** to **understand** than a **long list** of numbers. E.g.

> In a survey of 2000 households, 1384 used their kettle three times a day, and 416 used it more than 6 times daily.

> More than two thirds of households use their kettle three times a day. About one in five use it more than 6 times daily.

Here, the raw data has been turned into statistics.

Evidence & Examples

Examples illustrate Reasons

1) **Examples** support reasons because they **illustrate** them with a description of a **real situation** where they're **true**.

> Auntie Ethel is finding it hard to move around her house. Last week, she couldn't manage the stairs and had to sleep in the sitting room. She should move into sheltered accommodation.

This example makes the reason "Auntie Ethel is finding it hard to move around her house" more convincing, by describing an actual occasion where it's true.

2) **Examples** usually only describe **one situation**, so they're too **specific** to effectively **support** a broad **conclusion**.

3) **Strong** arguments use examples to make **reasons** more **developed** and **convincing**, but **not** as reasons themselves.

4) Examples are also used to illustrate **evidence**. **Arguments** which have **evidence** and **examples** usually look a bit like this:

reason	•	Exercise is a very effective way to cope with arthritic pain.
evidence	•	Studies show that a 20% increase in physical activity can improve joint flexibility by more than 40%.
example	•	My Auntie Liz does yoga every day, and her arthritis never bothers her.
conclusion	•	The NHS should provide classes and schemes encouraging exercise for arthritis sufferers.

Ricky illustrated his argument with an example of a powerful karate slap.

Examples and Evidence are not Reasons

1) In common notation, evidence is '**Ev**' and examples are '**Ex**'.

2) Usually, **common notation** shows evidence and examples as **less important** than the reasons and conclusion.

3) This is because they're not **essential** to the argument's **structure**. Evidence and examples are **not** extra **reasons** — **without** them the argument would **still work**.

E.g:

R1	•	There's too many folk overfed
+ Ev	•	studies suggest it's widespread
+ Ex	•	I knew someone who ate 'til he got stuck in a gate
C	•	therefore start eating salad instead

Phrases that often indicate evidence in an argument include — 'for example' and 'such as'.

Practice Questions

Q1   What is the purpose of evidence in an argument?

Q2   Name three different kinds of research that might be included as evidence. Give an example of each one.

Exam Question

Q1   Identify one example and one other kind of evidence in the paragraph below.   [4 marks]

> "We send our children to school when they're too young. Four-year-olds need time to play — they should be making dens and climbing trees. Our mad policy of pushing toddlers into the classroom has many negative consequences. Robert Medwell, in his research paper on Educational Improvement and Reform, notes that "by the time a child reaches fifteen, he has been in education for over a decade. It isn't surprising that this leads to boredom and bad behaviour". Furthermore, there is no evidence of the benefit of schooling from age four. I started school when I was six, and I turned out fine."

"I dislike arguments of any kind. They're always vulgar, and often convincing"*

Ol' Wildey wouldn't like an argument full of examples and evidence then — because an argument with evidence, nine times out of ten, will be more convincing than an argument without. If only there were more vulgar examples, that'd be more entertaining... Anyways, you'd better make sure you know all the different kinds of evidence, cos you can bet it'll come up later on as well.

Evaluating Evidence

Remember all the different kinds of evidence? Now you need to know how to evaluate them. The fun just never ends...

Evaluating Evidence means Deciding if it's Useful

1) The **Unit 1** exam will have **questions** about **evaluating evidence** — these two pages cover all you need to know.

2) Questions about evaluating evidence usually **start** with the word "**explain**". E.g. a question might ask you to explain **how** a piece of evidence "**gives support**" to an argument or **why** it only offers "**limited support**".

3) Here are the things you need to consider when looking at evidence:

Researchers need to survey a Reasonable Proportion

E.g. | 82% of teenagers in Borisville think fish, chips and mushy peas is a balanced meal (based on a survey of 100 teenagers).

1) When you **first** read the example above, 82% sounds like **a lot** of teenagers.

2) But you need to remember that it's **not** 82% of **all** teenagers — it's 82% of **all the teenagers** who were **surveyed**.

3) The teenagers who were surveyed are called the **sample**. This sample consists of **100 teenagers**.

4) Whether or not 100 teenagers is a **reasonable proportion** depends on **how many** teenagers live in Borisville. If there are only **1000** teenagers living there, 100 is a reasonable proportion. But if **half a million** teenagers live there, the sample size is **too small** and so the results of the survey can't be used as **reliable** evidence.

5) If the **sample** used to support statements about a **large** population is **too small**, it's called **over-generalisation**.

Evidence needs to be Representative

Representative means it gives a reliable picture of the whole group being talked about.

Research has found that 78% of students now have a car — so councils should stop providing free bus passes for students.

1) The percentage in this survey is being used to make a claim about **all** students — so the sample used should be **representative**. This means including students from different:

- economic backgrounds
- geographic backgrounds
- ethnicities
- religious groups

2) The **methods** used to gather a sample can **affect** how **representative** it is. For example:
- If students were surveyed at the **bus stop**, a lot of students asked probably **wouldn't have cars**.
- But if the survey was posted on a **car insurance** website, it's **likely** that the respondents would all **have cars**.
- The survey would be **most representative** if it was carried out in a **variety** of places.

3) If you're asked to say how representative **one person's views** are of a **group** then you need to look out for **similarities** between that **person** and the group as a **whole**. E.g. does that person **know** more or less about the situation than the rest of the group, are they the same **gender**, are they the same **age**? **Don't** just say 'it's only one person's opinion'.

Statistics can be Interpreted in Different Ways

Statistics (see p.12) can be **misleading**, because people tend to use the **interpretation** that **best suits** their argument. E.g.

Crime Data from 2009 & 2010 for Tuckden Village (pop. 1000)					
2009			**2010**		
Type of Crime	No. incidents	Value of goods stolen (£)	Type of Crime	No. incidents	Value of good stolen (£)
Mugging	2	95, 580	Mugging	6	35, 50, 120, 120, 120, 125
Burglary	5	445, 580, 580, 580, 600	Burglary	5	120, 450, 500, 500, 545
Car theft	3	1335, 1895, 3100	Car theft	4	4995, 5500, 5600, 7430

Argument A
Tuckden village is becoming a lawless nightmare. There has been an enormous 50% rise in crime rates, and it's not just teen rascals pinching petty cash. The average amount stolen in an incidence of theft has increased from £979 to £1747.

*These examples contain different figures because they've used different methods to interpret the data. Argument A states the **mean** amount that's been stolen, and Argument B states the **mode** amount. See p.43 for more about mean and mode.*

Argument B
Yes, there has been a small increase in crime: 1.5% of Tuckden residents have been victim of some kind of theft this year, compared to 1% in 2009. But the average value of goods stolen has fallen — from £580 to £120. We're not dealing with mobsters and crime lords.

Evaluating Evidence

Evidence should be Relevant

When evaluating **evidence**, you should look at how it's **linked** to
the **reason** and how well it **supports** the reason. For example:

> The average British family doesn't make the effort to eat healthily
> anymore. Studies show that 71% of families regularly eat dinner in
> front of the television, instead of whilst talking around the dinner table.

*...and now for something
completely irrelevant...*

The studies tell us **where** families are more likely to eat, but this has
nothing to do with **what** they are eating and **how healthy** it is. All
these families could be eating salads in front of the television —
so the evidence is **not relevant** to the reason.

Evidence can be Interpreted in Different ways

1) People often choose to **interpret** evidence in a way that **supports** their argument.

2) But there might be a **more likely interpretation** for the evidence,
   which does not support their argument in the same way.

3) Evidence which has several possible meanings is **ambiguous**.

> For her last film, Carmel Hoverfork earned £12 million,
> making her the highest paid actress of 2010. This proves
> that she is the most talented actress of today.

4) The **explanation** given in the argument above **might** be true, but there could be **other** explanations — such as:

   - Carmel Hoverfork is the actress with the most demanding agent.
   - She is today's most popular actress, which guarantees the highest
     ticket sales, so directors will pay more to have her in their films.

Practice Questions

Q1   A make-up advert claims "92% of British women think our products are fabulous (based on a survey of 50 women)."
      Why is this evidence weak?

Q2   A cat-hater argues that "cats ruin your love life. 79% of dog-owners are married, compared to 53% of cat-owners".
      Give one other possible explanation for this evidence.

Exam Question

Q1   Evaluate two of the pieces of evidence used in the argument below.   [4 marks]

> "We need to bring good old-fashioned values back. For one thing, our society respects pointless
> competitiveness more than the vital skills of care-giving and medical knowledge. The average nurse earns
> £31,000 a year, whilst the highest paid footballer earned 29.6 million pounds last year. Also, there's no sense
> of community. My neighbours are very anti-social and have both grown really high hedges. A recent survey
> found that the majority of people know more about TV soap characters than their next-door neighbour."

There are three kinds of lies — lies, damned lies, and statistics...

*Use the steely daggers of evaluation on this page to make sure you don't get caught in an argument's sticky web of persuasive
evidence... Or just learn the techniques and apply them in the appropriate manner. Depends on how adventurous you're feeling I
suppose. Either way, look out for tricky statistics. If they're not explained in detail, be suspicious... very suspicious...*

Providing Extra Reasons

The exam has a few tricky looking questions — have a look through these pages so you know what questions to expect and how to tackle them. Warning: if you don't read these pages, you may run screaming in panic from the exam hall.

You might have to provide **Extra Reasons** to **Support** an **Argument**

In the exam, you might be given an **argument** and asked to provide **extra reasons** that would **support** its **conclusion**.

> The Internet enables socially awkward people to talk to others with similar interests in chatrooms and make new friends. This opportunity for companionship brings a lot of happiness to people. The Internet also provides more opportunities for small businesses to reach a larger audience of potential customers, so independent retailers have found happiness through increased success. Therefore, the Internet makes people happier by providing more opportunities.

This is the conclusion — its key points are:
- *The Internet provides more **opportunities**.*
- *These opportunities make people **happier**.*

> **Q1** In the argument above, the author argues that the Internet makes people happier by providing more opportunities. Give **one** reason of your own that supports this claim. [3 marks]

1) Pick out the reasons **already given in the argument**, so you don't **repeat** something that's already been said.
2) Then identify the **conclusion** and think **carefully** about it — it might have two or more different **key points**.
3) Make sure you give reasons that are **relevant** to each of the **key points**.

Here are some Dos and Don'ts

- Don't **rephrase** a reason that's already in the text.

> The Internet has helped boost profits for all kinds of businesses, through wide-reaching ad campaigns.

You can quote evidence or information from the text to support your new reason — just make sure the reason you give is definitely different from the reasons already there.

- Don't write something that **isn't relevant** to the conclusion's **main points**.

> Some people are so used to browsing the Internet every day that they can't go without it for more than 24 hours.

- This reason is relevant but **weak** — it supports a **part** of the conclusion but **not all of it**.

> The Internet provides the opportunity to easily research and learn about anything you want.

- To make the reason stronger, **combine** it with **another point** so that the two points **work together** to support the **whole** of the conclusion:

> The Internet provides the opportunity to easily research and learn about anything you want, and people can derive great happiness by increasing their knowledge in this way.

- But **remember** that the question only asks for **one reason**. If you go overboard and give a reason, intermediate conclusion and example you'll be **marked down**. It looks like you **don't know** the difference between reasons, examples and conclusions.

> The Internet provides the opportunity to easily research and learn about anything you want. Therefore, people have increased their knowledge so this makes them happier. For example, I now know about aardvark mating rituals and the definition of zoophilism, and I feel very happy.

There's a worked answer for a question like this on p.69.

Identifying Whether Reasons Support Conclusions

One of the most important questions you'll ever ask — even more important than "How much wood would a woodchuck chuck if a woodchuck could chuck wood?" — is "Do these reasons support the conclusion?" Here's how to answer it...

You'll be asked to Assess how Strongly a Conclusion is Supported by the Reasons

1) You'll probably get a **question** in the exam which asks you to "Assess how **strongly** these reasons **support** the conclusion" — or something similar.

2) This just means writing about how **strongly** the reasons and conclusion are **linked**.

3) You **won't** be asked to say if the argument is strong or weak **overall**. All you need to do is pick out **some** of its **strengths** and **weaknesses** (see p.37).

4) There's a worked answer to this kind of question on p.69.

Warning: rubbing your argument in baby oil and dressing it in a thong won't make it stronger.

Reasons need to be Relevant

1) Don't assume that just because an argument has lots of reasons that the conclusion must be well-supported. The argument might contain just a **few relevant reasons** and a lot of **irrelevant** ones.

2) It's easy to **think** a reason is relevant when it **isn't** really — especially if the reason is on the same **general topic** as the conclusion.

3) But to be **relevant**, reasons must be about **precisely** the same thing as the conclusion.

4) In the example below, the reasons need to be about **violent** video games and how it's the **government's** responsibility to ban them.

R1 is **relevant** because it gives a reason to accept that a petition should be sent to the government, rather than to anyone else.

> We should send a petition to the British government, asking them to ban violent video games in our country. After all, it is their duty to do everything in their power to keep children safe from harm. Video games are so popular that some studies have shown that Super Mario is more recognisable to children than Mickey Mouse.

R2 is about the **general** topic of video games — but it's not about **violent** video games, or why the government should ban them, so it's **irrelevant**.

5) A **reason** can still be **relevant** if it's only linked to **one part** of the **conclusion** — it doesn't have to be linked to **every** part. But the argument **also** needs to contain reasons **relevant** to the **other** parts of the conclusion — otherwise the conclusion is **weakly** supported. More on this on the next page...

Practice Questions

Q1   Which of these reasons is relevant to the conclusion "Therefore, it is very probable that aliens exist"?
a) 'ET' was a great film   b) If aliens existed it would be really cool   c) The universe is vast and full of possibilities.

Q2   Which of these is not a sign of a strongly supported conclusion?
a) All the reasons are relevant   b) The argument hasn't got many weaknesses   c) The argument has lots of reasons.

Exam Question

Q1   Suggest **one** extra reason to support the conclusion of the argument below.   [3 marks]

Teenagers tend to have mood swings and sulk a lot, but if they volunteered to help others less fortunate than themselves they might get some perspective and realise how lucky they are. Also, young adults have a bad reputation as vandals and hooligans — if more of them volunteered to do charitable work, their reputation would improve. Therefore, more teenagers should volunteer to do charitable work.

WonderReasons — now with reinforced straps and underwiring for extra support...

If you're asked to assess how strongly reasons support a conclusion, don't panic. Just remember these questions to get you going — What are the conclusion's key points? Are the reasons relevant? Do they cover all the conclusion's key points? What the heck are sea monkeys anyway? Ok, maybe not that last one. No one knows the answer to that... damn those wiggly enigmas of nature...

Identifying Whether Reasons Support Conclusions

Here are some more lovely things to think about when you're assessing reasons...

All Parts of the Conclusion need to be Supported

1) The **conclusion** of the argument below is "we should petition the government to ban violent video games". To **strongly support** this conclusion, there must be reasons supporting the idea of a **petition**, the idea that **violent video games** need to be **banned**, and the point that the petition needs to be **sent** to the **government**.

> Our government is not doing enough to protect our children from violent video games. One of its key roles is to help children grow up to be friendly and responsible members of society. As concerned citizens, it is our duty to remind the government when it is neglecting this vital task. Therefore, we should petition the government to ban violent video games. After all, an Internet petition is the best way to establish general public support because it reaches a wide audience, and allows you to voice your concerns from the comfort of your own home. It's an effective and easy way of expressing our views to the government.

2) The point that says "we should **petition**" is supported by the reason that says it's "the best way to establish general public support". The point that the petition should be sent to the **government** is supported by the reasons that one of the government's "key roles is to help children grow up to be friendly" and "it is neglecting this vital task".

3) But there aren't **any reasons** to persuade us that **violent video games** are a **problem**.

4) So the conclusion as a **whole** is **not** strongly supported because **part** of it has no reasons supporting it at all.

Reasoning should be Consistent

1) If two reasons can't both be true at the same time it is called **inconsistent reasoning** (see p.36).

2) **Inconsistent** reasoning is **weak** — you can't accept **all** the reasons, so you **can't accept** the conclusion.

3) Here's an example of inconsistent reasoning:

> *Here the author claims that you cannot assume something is good just because it is natural...*

> Some people argue that it's natural for children to play aggressively, and if you take away violent video games they'll just pick up sticks and pretend to be shooting guns. But just because aggression is natural doesn't mean it's a good thing.
> Video games are also showing signs of being addictive. There have been reports of children spending over 12 hours a day in a darkened room, talking to no one, just staring at a flickering screen. That is just not natural.

> *... but here they assume something is bad because it is not natural.*

Language also needs to be Consistent

1) **Conflation** is when the person arguing uses **two words** as if they mean the **same thing**, when they actually **don't**.

> *R1 makes a claim about feelings of aggression.*

> Exposure to violent video games causes an increase in feelings of aggression in stressful situations. Aggressive behaviour in stressful situations often leads to incidents of fights and physical abuse, so a ban on violent video games would help decrease rates of violent crime.

> *R2 makes a claim about aggressive behaviour.*

> *We look at conflation again on p.50.*

2) The **first** sentence says that violent video games cause aggressive **feelings**. Then the **second** sentence goes on to talk about aggressive **behaviour**, as if they're the same thing.

3) It's a **subtle** difference, but they're actually **not** the **same** thing. You **might** argue that feelings of aggression **lead to** aggressive behaviour, but the **argument** doesn't do this — it just uses the two terms as if they mean the **same** thing.

Weak Reasoning often relies on Questionable Assumptions

1) Many arguments contain **assumptions** (see p.10-11). This in itself **doesn't weaken** the argument.

2) But an **assumption** can **weaken** an argument if it's **not** something most people would **agree** with.

> *This relies on the assumption that computer viruses are bad — which is generally agreed to be true.*

> Banning video games would increase the spread of computer viruses, because more people would download games illegally. Therefore the government shouldn't ban them.

> Violent video games provide an outlet for aggression. It's natural for youths to be aggressive, so the government should encourage the use of violent video games.

> *This relies on the assumption that something should be encouraged just because it's natural — but a lot of people would disagree with this.*

Identifying Whether Reasons Support Conclusions

Finally, embrace success like an old friend by making sure you know what to expect from the exam questions, knowing how to avoid all the common mistakes, and getting lots of practice...

Always **Refer** to the **Example** in your **Answer**

1) If you're asked to **assess** an argument, don't write a **long list** of what makes arguments **weak** or **strong** in general.

2) Discuss the argument **in the example** they have given you, and give **quotes** to back up your points.

3) It's a good idea to consider both **strengths** and **weaknesses** (see p.37) when you're assessing an argument.

Read the argument given below. Assess how strongly the conclusion is supported by the reasons. [6 marks]

"Occasionally, people who behave antisocially due to mental illness have been given ASBOs, which seems wrong. However, apart from a few exceptions, ASBOs have been very useful. Until now, policemen had to put up with a lot of disobedient behaviour, including people ignoring their requests and childish displays of sarcasm and backchat. The introduction of ASBOs has allowed the police to put a stop to antisocial behaviour, so all those people can now be punished. Therefore, ASBOs have been a complete success."

Weak arguments often have broad conclusions that are not fully supported by the reasons. If a conclusion is broad then it will be easier to challenge. Reasons must be relevant to the conclusion, otherwise they don't support it.

The argument conflates disobedient behaviour and antisocial behaviour. This means there is no reason to accept that "all those people can now be punished" for their **disobedient** behaviour just because police can now "put a stop to **antisocial** behaviour". The reasoning is also inconsistent. It states that there are "a few **exceptions**" to the success of ASBOs, so this is inconsistent with the conclusion that "ASBOs have been a **complete** success".

Practice Questions

Q1 What is conflation?

Q2 Identify one example of weak reasoning in the paragraph below, and explain why it is weak.

> "Children will really enjoy family theatre like musical pantomimes because it encourages audience participation. Also, the slapstick comedy will really appeal to their youthful sense of humour. Therefore, theatre is the perfect way to entertain your children as well as encouraging their creativity."

Exam Question

Q1 Read the argument below. Assess how successfully the reasons support the conclusion. You should make at least two developed points and directly refer to how the reasons link to the conclusion. [6 marks]

"Today's obsession with university degrees is making it harder to succeed in life. Companies used to employ people at sixteen or eighteen and train them on the job. Today, jobs haven't changed very much, but all applicants now have to have a university degree. It's also expensive to go to university, so this discriminates against many talented young people from poorer backgrounds.

This obsession also forces young people to waste three years of their lives studying for a degree that has no real relevance to the job they'll actually end up doing. Nobody goes to university for the right reasons anymore — students chase grades rather than enjoying education for its own sake.

A degree is not a guarantee of success in life. But we're led to believe that having a degree is more important than learning practical skills such as effective relationship-building, crisis-solving and proper planning. Finally, people who go to university learn to think in exactly the same way as all the other graduates. This actually makes it less likely that they will come up with the original and inspirational insights and ideas on which success is often built."

I like my arguments like I like my Christmas cake — made with lots of raisins

Dum-dumdum-di-dum-daahhh — and so we've arrived at the end of Section One. Hurrah. If you haven't turned into Sherlock Holmes by now, inspecting every paragraph with a magnifying glass and a trusty-if-dull sidekick, then we've clearly failed in our Critical Thinking mission. Get yourself a deer-stalker hat and a pipe, and get back to the beginning of the section. Pip pip.

Plausibility

Welcome to Section Two. It's all about credibility — whether you can believe something or not. My Gran always says, "Never believe a right-footed penguin," which is good advice, but not terribly useful. This section's much more helpful.

A **Claim** is a **Statement** that can be **Challenged**

1) In AS Critical Thinking you'll talk about **claims** — **statements** people make that it's possible to **question** or **disagree** with.

2) An argument's **reasons** and **conclusions** (see p.4) are both types of **claim**.

An **Event** or **Outcome** is **Plausible** if it's **Likely** to happen

It was unlikely that Tyson would win the 'Most Beautiful Baby' contest.

1) **Some** claims are about future events or outcomes, e.g.

> Cutting the health budget will mean people waiting longer for operations.

2) A **likely** event is **more** plausible, an **unlikely** one is **less** plausible.

> Tomorrow the Queen will break the triple-jump world record.

This event **isn't very plausible** — it's very **unlikely** that this could ever happen.

> Raising the speed limit will cause more car accidents.

This outcome is very **plausible** — it's **likely** that this will happen.

A **Claim** is **Plausible** if it's **Reasonable**

> The words 'plausible' and 'reasonable' are both used in exam questions — they mean the same thing.

1) A **plausible** claim is one that **could** be true — it's **reasonable** to believe it.

> Cabbage is healthier than chocolate.

This claim is **plausible** — it's **reasonable** to believe it.

> 100% of people prefer cabbage to chocolate.

This claim is **not very plausible**. It's not **reasonable** to say that all people prefer one thing to another — it just doesn't happen.

2) Just because a claim is **plausible**, that doesn't mean it's definitely **true**. You're just making a **judgement** based on the **information** you have available at the **time**.

It's plausible to say...
> Crime rates have risen by 5% this year.

... but you might find out **later** from police reports that this **information** is wrong.

In the **Exam** you'll have to judge **How Plausible** claims or outcomes are

1) In the Unit 1 exam you'll probably get a question on **plausibility** that looks a bit like this:

> Q1 Refer to the documents provided and make a judgement as to whether speed cameras have a positive or negative effect on the rate of car accidents. You should make your judgement based on the relative plausibility (likelihood) of both outcomes.

2) The question's asking you to **compare** the **likelihood** that speed cameras will have a **positive** effect with the **likelihood** that they'll have a **negative** effect.

3) You need to **conclude** that one effect is **more** likely (more plausible) than the other.

4) **Sometimes** you'll get a question which **only** asks you to say how plausible **one effect** is:

> Q2 Assess the plausibility of this claim, with reference to material from the passage.

> 'Assess' means discuss **one** side, e.g. what makes the claim **plausible**, discuss the **other** side, e.g what makes it **less plausible**, and then add a **conclusion** about how plausible you think it is **overall**.

Credibility

A claim is **Credible** if it can be **Believed**

1) As well as deciding if claims are **plausible**, you'll need to be able to say how **credible** they are — how far we should **believe** them.

2) Even if a claim is **plausible**, there might be **other reasons** why you should or shouldn't believe it.

3) One way to help you decide is to assess the **credibility** of the **person** or **organisation** who made the claim.

4) If the **source** is **credible**, then the **claims** the source makes will be credible **too**.

Last year I went on holiday with John and we went skiing.

- This claim is **plausible** — it's not unreasonable to think that it could have happened.
- But if you know that I always lie about my holidays, you might decide that it isn't **credible**.

5) Remember — a claim that is plausible **and** credible can still be **false**.

In the **Exam** you'll be asked about the **Credibility** of **Source Material**

1) In the exam, questions about **credibility** might ask you to judge the credibility of an **individual**, an **organisation**, a **document**, or a **claim**. All of these things can **also** be referred to as a **source**.

2) When you assess a **document** or a **claim**, write about the credibility of its **writer** or the **organisation** *See p.32 for examples.*
that's published it. If the **writer / organisation** is not very credible, then their **claims / documents** won't be very credible — just remember to **refer** back to the **claim** or **document** in your answer.

3) There are **two** main **types of question** you might get on credibility:

Q1 Refer to Source 3. Assess how far the <u>claims of the human rights campaigner</u> are credible.

In this question, '**assess**' means **discuss** and make a **judgement** about the credibility of just **one person**.

Q2 Look at Document 2. Decide whether the bypass will affect the local area in a positive or negative way. Make your case based on <u>the relative credibility of the two sides</u> of the debate.

Making a case based on the **relative credibility** of two sides means **comparing** how credible they **each** are.

You work out **How Credible** a source is using **Credibility Criteria**

1) To help you **decide** how credible a source is, there are **seven** things for you to **look out** for.

2) These seven things are called **credibility criteria**. There's **more** about them on the next 8 pages.

3) You won't have to use **all** these criteria at once — you'll probably be asked to **decide which** ones to use, and say how each of them **strengthens** or **weakens** the source's credibility.

Practice Questions

Q1   What is a claim?

Q2   What is the difference between plausibility and credibility?

Exam Question

Q1   Assess the relative plausibility of these two claims. Explain your reasoning.
a)   Over-fishing in the North Sea is one of the biggest environmental problems facing the UK today.
b)   There are no fish left in the North Sea, due to over-fishing.   [5 marks]

These pages are just unbelievably incredible...

It's easy to confuse plausibility and credibility but you've got to know the difference. Once you've learnt these two pages you can start dropping phrases like, 'That's plausible...' and, 'She's quite credible...' casually into conversation. People will stare in wonderment at your wisdom and gasp in disbelief at your cleverness. Or not. Either way, you'll be well prepared for the exam.

Bias

Now it's time to get a grip on those pesky credibility criteria. The next 8 pages will explain each one, and then pages 30-33 will show you how to use them. I'd like to say it's more exciting than it sounds, but you probably wouldn't believe me...

Bias *is being* Prejudiced *towards* One Side *of an argument*

1) Bias affects how people **see** an issue. People may be biased because of **beliefs** and **opinions** they **already** have.

2) A biased person often **doesn't know** they're biased, and doesn't necessarily **mean** to be. Bias can be **subconscious**.

> Sally suspects the kids next door of stealing her milk because they're always scruffily dressed.

> Sally has no **evidence** that the kids are guilty — she's **biased** against them because they **look** a certain way.

> **Bias** may make people **prejudiced** for or against a certain point of view.

People can be Biased *because of their* Background *or* Experiences

1) People often have **different** opinions or perspectives because of their **background** and the **experiences** they've had.

2) These **opinions** can make them biased towards or against **one side** of an argument, or the **person** making it.

3) Here are **some** of the things that can **cause** people to be biased:

Religious beliefs	Past experience	Family/Friends
A woman votes for a politician because he shares the same religious beliefs.	A retired teacher on the town council argues that the majority of their budget should be spent on schools.	A judge chooses her best friend's restaurant as the winner of a contest.
She chooses who to vote for based on **religion**, not on his **political** views.	His **teaching experience** may make him see the needs of schools as the council's main **priority**.	Perhaps she thinks **more positively** about her friend's restaurant because of their **relationship**.

4) If we **suspect** that someone might be biased, it usually **decreases** their **credibility** — we're less likely to believe them because this **bias** could give them a **motive** to exaggerate, distort evidence, or even lie.

Biased *arguments often put forward only* One Side *of a debate*

1) One way to **spot bias** is to check whether people have only given **one** point of view and **left out** information that **disagrees** with their point — whether they've used facts **selectively**.

> This resident **only** puts forward **his own** point of view — his account is **biased** against speed bumps.

> Local resident Carson Driver said, "Speed bumps are an annoyance for drivers all over the country. They don't do anything so they should all be removed." The Mayor of Woodforton replied, "Speed bumps are expensive and sometimes they do irritate drivers. However, we install them on roads where they are needed to slow down traffic in order to make our children safer. Each street needs to be considered independently."

See p.14-15 for more on misleading evidence.

> The Mayor considers **both** sides of the argument — his account is **unbiased** and balanced.

2) In the **exam**, look out for sources that are **one-sided** — they might contain **bias** which would **decrease** their credibility.

Vested Interest

Vested Interest can lead to *Biased* claims

1) If a person or organisation has a **vested interest** in the outcome of an argument, they'll **gain** something from it going their way — e.g. money, power, reputation, career prospects etc.

> A bike manufacturer might try to convince the council to build more cycle routes in big cities. If cycling on the road was safer then more people might buy their bikes.

2) A person or organisation **also** has a vested interest if the argument going their way allows them to **avoid** something **negative** — e.g. financial loss, damage to their reputation, criminal charges etc.

> People living near the site of a proposed new nuclear power station might have a vested interest in opposing the plans — if it were built, it could reduce the value of their houses.

Jewellers quickly realised they had a vested interest in promoting this particular fashion.

3) Vested interest has a similar effect to **bias** — it gives people a **motive** for putting forward **one-sided** arguments.

4) This means that, like bias, vested interest can **decrease** the **credibility** of a source or witness.

> An employee accuses his rival of stealing from the company a week before a promotion is announced.

This employee wants to be **promoted** instead of his rival. This vested interest **decreases** the credibility of his accusation.

5) If the person or organisation on **one side** of an argument has a **vested interest**, it doesn't **automatically** make them **less credible** than the person or organisation arguing against them.

6) Other credibility criteria might **increase** their credibility, or there might be criteria which **decrease** the credibility of the **other** side of the argument.

Vested interest doesn't **Always Decrease** *credibility*

1) If someone has a lot to **lose** from being caught lying, they have a vested interest in telling the **truth**.

2) This **increases** the **credibility** of their claims — it gives us more **reason to believe** them.

In these examples, the person or organisation has a vested interest in telling the **truth**:

> A newspaper breaking an important news story.

> A doctor in court describing a victim's injuries.

> A football referee explaining why he's given a penalty.

3) **Any** person or organisation whose career or business **depends heavily** on their reputation for **impartiality** and **fairness**, like those in the examples above, will have a **vested interest** in telling the **truth**.

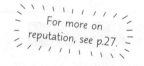
For more on reputation, see p.27.

You need to be able to **Explain** *how a* **Vested Interest** *affects* **Credibility**

1) It's no good just **telling** the examiner that someone has a vested interest.

2) You need to give **details** about how this affects their **credibility** — whether we're more or less **likely** to **believe** them.

3) When you're **writing** about someone with a vested interest, ask yourself these **questions**:

- What **side** of the argument (if any) are they likely to support?
- What do they stand to **gain**? (Or what do they stand to **lose**?)
- Does this vested interest make them **more** or **less credible**?

Neutrality

Neutrality is the Opposite of Bias

1) A **neutral** source or witness isn't **prejudiced** in favour of or against **either** side of an argument.

2) They're **not biased** and they don't have any **vested interest**.

On the exam paper you might see the word 'impartial' instead of 'neutral'.

> Neutrality **always increases** credibility.

3) A neutral source is **always** more credible than a **biased** one because they have no **motive** to exaggerate, lie or distort evidence.

4) Just because a source is **neutral**, that doesn't mean they'll be the **most credible** option. They might go against other **neutral** accounts, or there might be other **factors** that damage their credibility.

   E.g. A passer-by who saw an armed robbery may be **neutral**, but if they were standing at a distance on a dark night, their account might not be as **credible** as that of someone who had a better view.

5) It can be pretty tricky to find **completely** neutral sources — some people think we're **all** at least **slightly** biased.

Neutral sources are Balanced or aren't linked to Either Side of the argument

1) Neutral sources either:

Present a balanced account	Have no links to either side
• They present accounts that aren't **biased** towards either side. • They don't try to mislead people by **leaving out** any relevant information.	• If someone's neutral they're not **linked** to either side of an argument by their beliefs or people they know. • They have nothing to gain or lose from taking a particular side — they have no **vested interest**.

   E.g. A journalist writes a review of a new digital radio. He has no links to the radio's manufacturer, and he gives a balanced account of the performance of the radio, mentioning good points and bad points. He is **neutral**.

2) Neutral sources can be used in a **biased** way. Neutral evidence can be **manipulated**, or used **selectively** to put across only **one** side of an argument.   The manufacturer of the radio uses the journalist's review in its adverts. It only uses the positive quotes, and leaves out the negative ones.

Practice Questions

Q1   What is the difference between bias and vested interest?

Q2   What two characteristics can neutral sources have?

Exam Question

Q1   Refer to the text below. Make a judgement regarding the credibility of one claim made by Councillor Manson, and one claim made by Professor Samuels. Apply one credibility criterion to each claim and explain how it strengthens or weakens the claim.
[7 marks]

"Oil from the stricken tanker *Midnight* has hit the beaches at Rainton-on-Sea. The Mayor, Councillor Manson, said, "People should not cancel their holidays at Rainton, because the oil will be cleared up very quickly". However, the marine biologist, Professor Samuels, claims that, "It could take up to three months to clear the beaches, and many fish and seabirds could die."

I collect thermal underwear — you might call it a vest-ed interest...

This might all sound like a foreign language at the moment, but it does get easier with practice. Try reading an article on a news website or in a newspaper and look out for the sources they've used. Write down which ones you think are biased, neutral or have a vested interest and why you think that. This'll be great practice for making judgements about source material in the exam.

Experience & Expertise

In an argument, it helps if your view is backed up by someone who knows what they're talking about. Experts are people who really know their stuff — the next few pages will tell you what makes them experts, and how being an expert affects their credibility...

Experience and Expertise are Not the Same thing

1) Often the **sources** you'll get in the exam will contain **quotes** or **opinions** from people who know a **lot** about the subject they're discussing.

2) These sources have either **experience**, or **expertise**, or a combination of **both**.

> **Expertise** means specialist skills and training that give someone knowledge that most people don't have.

> **Experience** means knowledge gained from having done or encountered something, often over a long period of time.

> Mr. Clifford has lots of **expertise** on the subject of wind turbines.

> On Tuesday night, Bluebridge Town Council held a meeting to discuss whether the plans to build a wind farm on Blueberry Hill should be allowed to go ahead. At the meeting Mr. Clifford, the engineer who designed the turbines, stated that, "The farm will cause a maximum of 35 decibels of noise as measured from the nearest houses, which is an acceptable level according to government guidelines." Mrs. Clare, who has lived in the shadow of a similar wind farm for five years, disagreed. "The kids are up and down all night," she claimed, "they can't sleep through all the whirring noises. It's even worse on stormy nights."

> Mrs. Clare has **experience** that is relevant to the case.

3) You'll often be given **extra information** such as job titles or qualifications to help you **spot** if someone has particular expertise or experience, e.g.

- Mr. Clifford, the engineer who designed the turbines...
- Dr. Frances, from the University of Melton Mowbray...
- Mrs. Clare, who has lived in the shadow of a similar wind farm for five years...
- Sally Hornchurch, a stamp collector for the last forty-five years...

Experience and Expertise can Increase Credibility

1) A claim made by a source with specialist **expertise** or **experience** is usually quite **credible** — because of their **experience** or **training**, they are likely to know more than **most** people about their subject.

2) Here are some **examples** of experts you might come across:

- Doctors
- Lawyers
- Army officers
- Police officers
- Teachers
- Scientists

Trevor's expertise in digger decoration was a rare and unappreciated skill.

Experience or Expertise must be Relevant

1) A source's experience or expertise **must** be **relevant** to the argument.

2) If it's **not** relevant, it **won't** increase the **credibility** of any claim they make.

3) Someone with expertise or experience in **one field** might **not** be **qualified** to comment on an issue in a **different field**, e.g.

> A surgeon's evidence is more credible on heart transplants than on how to erect scaffolding safely.

Experience & Expertise

Experts are often Neutral...

1) Normally, experts aren't **personally involved** in the argument they're commenting on.
2) Their accounts also tend to be **balanced** — they give **both sides** of the argument.
3) This means they're more **likely** to be **neutral**.
4) If an expert is **neutral**, then this **increases** their credibility (see p.24).

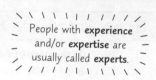

*People with **experience** and/or **expertise** are usually called **experts**.*

...but Not Always

1) Experts can be affected by **bias** or **vested interest** like anyone else.
2) Evidence from experts is **less** credible if it's **not** neutral.
3) When you're looking at a source containing an expert's opinion, ask yourself whether the expert has any **links** to either side and whether they've put forward a **balanced** point of view.

See p.24 for more on neutrality.

*Felicity Inkpen is an **expert** in fiction writing. This **increases** her credibility.*

Felicity Inkpen, the bestselling novelist and respected competition judge, has been questioned by the media about her decision to award the Green Medal for Fiction to Isabelle Franklin. Ms. Franklin's new novel, *Apples and Rhubarb*, is published by Inkpen Press, the company set up by Felicity Inkpen. Sales of the book are certain to increase now the prize has been announced, and it is Ms. Inkpen and her company who will enjoy the profits.

*Ms. Inkpen will **gain** money if Isabelle Franklin wins the prize — she has a **vested interest** so she isn't **neutral**. This **decreases** her credibility.*

Expert claims aren't Always the Most credible

1) If a claim is supported by **relevant** experience or expertise, it **increases** its credibility.
2) But **other** sources or witnesses might still be **more** credible.
3) This **might** be because:

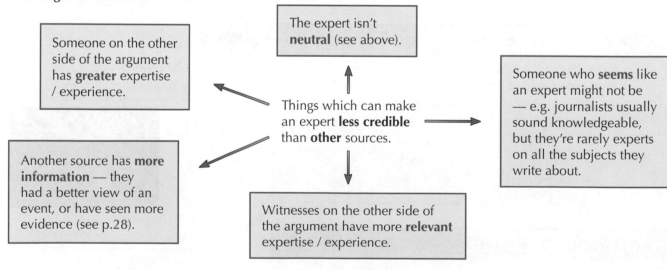

Someone on the other side of the argument has **greater** expertise / experience.

The expert isn't **neutral** (see above).

Someone who **seems** like an expert might not be — e.g. journalists usually sound knowledgeable, but they're rarely experts on all the subjects they write about.

Things which can make an expert **less credible** than **other** sources.

Another source has **more information** — they had a better view of an event, or have seen more evidence (see p.28).

Witnesses on the other side of the argument have more **relevant** expertise / experience.

4) In the exam you might be asked to say what **extra information** you need to be **sure** of a person or document's **credibility**. In the case of an **expert**, you might want to check:
   - That they have had **relevant** specialist **training** in the subject they're talking about.
   - That they haven't been in trouble before for **misrepresenting** information.
   - Who they're **paid** by or how the company they work for is **funded**.

See p.33 for more on giving extra information.

Reputation

Your *Reputation* is the *Opinion* people have of you

1) If someone has a **positive reputation** it **increases** their credibility.
If they have a **negative reputation**, it **decreases** their credibility.

2) A **person** or **organisation's** reputation might be based on their own **previous actions** —
e.g. whether they've usually been **truthful** or whether they've often told **lies** or distorted the truth.

3) **Groups** of people can also have reputations based on the **past actions** of their **members** — e.g. doctors
and policemen are **generally** considered trustworthy, but people are more suspicious of politicians.

4) Many people have a **vested interest** in maintaining a **positive** reputation —
e.g. a competition judge's **career** depends on people thinking that she's **fair**
so she has a **vested interest** in maintaining her **reputation** for fairness. This
would make her judgements more **credible** because she wouldn't want to
risk her job by **favouring** one of the contestants unfairly.

5) If someone has a **good reputation**, their view can help make an argument
more **credible** even if they're **not** an **expert**. E.g. a **vicar** might oppose
plans to knock down a leisure centre because he thinks it will increase
youth crime. People are more likely to **believe** him because although he
isn't an **expert** on youth crime or town planning, he has a good **reputation**.

Marie was certain she had a scoop when she spotted this man outside the supermarket

You need to be *Careful* when using *Reputation* to judge *Credibility*

Just because someone's acted **one** way in the past, that **doesn't** mean that they can't **change**.

Someone we accuse of lying because they've lied in the past might be telling the truth this time.

Some doctors have committed terrible crimes, and most politicians are honest.

When we judge a **group's** reputation, we're making a **generalisation**, but there are always **exceptions**.

Reputation isn't always **fair** — it might be based on **rumours** that aren't true or on **second-hand** evidence.

A celebrity might have a reputation for infidelity because of untrue rumours in the press.

A salesman may have a reputation for exaggerating when selling cars, but this doesn't necessarily affect his **credibility** as the witness of a murder.

You've got to think about the **relevance** of the reputation.

Practice Questions

Q1 What's the difference between experience and expertise?
Q2 Give three reasons why an expert might not be the most credible source.

Exam Question

Q1 Assess the credibility of the claims made by each of the people below. Apply one credibility
criterion to each source and explain how it strengthens or weakens the credibility of their claim. [9 marks]

Mr. James, an accountant: 'This bypass should not be allowed because it'll destroy local wildlife habitats.'
Miss Hubert, from the council's transport department: 'The bypass won't harm wildlife habitats — it'll be ecofriendly.'
Dr. Sandra Ford, a professor of biology and ecology: 'The bypass will have minimal impact on local ecosystems.'

I expect experienced experts examine examples excellently...

Experts are pretty easy to spot in source material — articles and documents often give an expert's qualifications, like "Dr. Cookey, Professor of Nutrition at Asquith University". In a debate about the benefits of biscuits you might be more likely to believe him than "Mrs. Smeggins from West Wisbury". Unless she has lots of experience in biscuit-related matters, of course...

Ability to See or Perceive

Well, we've come to the final two credibility criteria — then we've just got to cover how to use them. So put your seat backs and tray tables in the upright position and hold on tight. (Yeah, ok, that wasn't great but I'm doing my best... It's not easy you know.)

Someone's **Ability** to **See** or **Perceive** affects their **Credibility**

1) Someone who **witnesses** an event has **seen or perceived** it.
   E.g. a customer who is **inside** a bank when it is **robbed**.

2) **'Perceive'** means **experience** with any of the **senses** — not **just** the eyes.

> **Good** ability to see or perceive **always increases** credibility.

3) Having **access** to relevant **information** can also **affect** someone's ability to perceive. E.g. a **town councillor** in charge of granting planning permission has **access** to more **information** about new building developments than a local **resident**. Their **ability** to **see** this information **increases** their credibility.

Several factors can **Reduce** someone's **Ability** to **Perceive**

A **witness's** account will be **less** credible if:

- They didn't observe the **whole event** (e.g. they arrived after the event began or their view was obstructed).
- The **conditions** at the time reduced their ability to perceive the event (e.g. low light, fog, lots of noise).
- They were **distracted** by something else. (e.g. a phone conversation, another person).
- They were **affected** by drugs (e.g. alcohol, cannabis, medication).
- They were under physical or emotional **stress** (e.g. if they were afraid or in pain).
- They have a **medical condition or disability** which reduces their ability to observe or recall the event (e.g. memory loss or sight problems).
- They've **forgotten** some details in the time since the event (e.g. court cases can be months after an event).
- They didn't **understand** what was happening (e.g. a young child remembering a car accident).

There are **Two** types of **Evidence** you might see in the **Exam**:

Primary evidence is **First-Hand**....

1) If someone has **seen or perceived** an event then their account is **primary** — it's **first-hand** and **direct**.

> E.g. Sybil telling her neighbour Agnes about the dramatic arrest she's just seen outside the supermarket.

2) Even though **primary** evidence can be affected by the **factors** in the blue box above, it's usually **more credible** than **secondary** evidence.

...and **Secondary** evidence is **Second-Hand**

1) When someone reports **another person's** description of an event, but they didn't actually witness it for **themselves**, this is **secondary** evidence — it's **second-hand** and **indirect**.

> E.g. Agnes phoning her daughter and telling her Sybil's story about the arrest.

2) Secondary evidence is **less credible** because it often gets changed as it's retold by different people.

3) Agnes might **choose** which bits to tell her daughter if she's **biased** or has a **vested interest**. She might also **forget** some details, **add** in new ones or have a different **interpretation** of what happened during the arrest.

4) Second-hand evidence is sometimes called **hearsay**. Rumour and gossip are both **types** of hearsay.

Corroboration & Consistency

Corroboration *is when* Different Sources Agree

1) When two or more sources **say the same thing** (they agree) it's know as **corroboration**.

2) Corroboration **increases credibility**.

3) **But** sources which **corroborate** each other can still have their credibility affected by **other** factors, e.g.:

> Mike and Paul, Stephen's friends, told the headmaster that it was Josh who'd stolen the keys, not Stephen.

Mike and Paul's statements **corroborate** each other — they agree. But their **credibility** is affected by the fact that they might be **biased** towards their friend.

4) In the **exam** you might be given a claim and have to pick one it **corroborates**.

This claim... | "Closing this road will cause long traffic jams." | ...**corroborates** this claim... | "Traffic will get worse if this road is closed."

Accounts *are* Conflicting *if they* Disagree *with each other*

> Conflicting accounts are also described as 'inconsistent'.

1) **Conflict** is the **opposite** of corroboration.

2) Evidence from two sources is **conflicting** if they **disagree with** each other.
E.g. one person claims that speed cameras make roads safer, but another says they make them more dangerous.

3) Some sources **agree** on the **main** points, but **disagree** when it comes to the **detail**. Their credibility will then depend on how **important** these details are and **how many** differences there are.

> Mr. and Mrs. Redmond have witnessed an armed robbery. They agree on most things, but Mr. Redmond thinks the robber's hat was green, and Mrs. Redmond thinks it was blue.

Most of their claims **corroborate** each other so the witnesses seem **credible**. But if a blue hat is a major piece of **evidence**, the disagreement is more **important**.

Accounts *are* Consistent *if they* Don't Conflict

1) Two accounts that **don't contradict** each other are **consistent**, e.g.:

This claim... | "Closing this road will cause long traffic jams." | ...is **consistent** with this claim... | "This town has a huge traffic problem."

...but they don't **corroborate** each other as they describe different things.

2) If **all** the claims in a **single** account or piece of evidence can be true **at the same time**, like in the example above, we say it is **consistent** — it doesn't **contradict itself**.

3) An account or piece of evidence is **inconsistent** if it contains two claims that **contradict** each other — they can't both be true.

> **Consistent** accounts are **always more credible** than **inconsistent** ones.

The boys weren't consistent — they were definitely conflicting.

Practice Questions

Q1   Explain the difference between corroboration and consistency.

Exam Question

Q1   Assess how far Mr. Donaldson's evidence is credible. You should make one point and refer to a credibility criterion in your answer.   [3 marks]

"I was walking home from the pub with some friends on Friday night. We'd had a few drinks and we were laughing and joking around. Suddenly we heard the screech of brakes and a loud smash. We turned around and behind us we saw the crashed car. The driver can't have been looking where he was going."

These sausages are incredible — they're inconsistent and uncorroborated...

Don't turn over yet — first make sure you're happy with all of the credibility criteria we've talked about so far. The next four pages are full of useful hints and tips about how to use these criteria to answer exam questions so it's important that you understand them before you move on. If there are any you're not sure about, now's a really good time to look back at them...

Assessing Plausibility

We've reached the last four pages you need to know for Unit 1. This is the best bit as you finally get to use all those pesky credibility criteria to assess some credibility. I'd like to say I can feel your excitement but I can't.

Some questions will ask how *Plausible* a *Claim* or *Outcome* is

1) You need to be able to **assess** the **plausibility** (reasonableness) of a **claim** or **outcome**.

2) Remember: **assess** means saying which factors make the claim seem **more** plausible, which factors make it seem **less** plausible, and then **deciding** how plausible it seems **overall**.

3) You can use **information** from the document to **help** you, but you'll have to include your **own ideas** too.

> The Prime Minister is considering the suggestion that all police officers in the UK should carry guns. Maggie James, from the Wives of Police Officers Association, has voiced her support for the plan saying, "Insisting that all police officers carry guns will keep them safer on the streets — they need to defend themselves against dangerous criminal gangs."
>
> However, critics of the plan have suggested that it will actually increase gun crime. The journalist Harrison Denton argues: "Increasing the number of guns on the streets of the UK, whether in the hands of the police or of criminals, also increases the risk to the public."
>
> The Minister of Justice put forward his view in a statement this morning: "It is true that in some areas, police need to carry firearms in order to carry out their duties properly. However, in leafy villages where crime rates are low, it makes no sense to have police officers carrying guns around everywhere — guns just aren't needed in many areas."

> Q1 Assess the reasonableness of the claim: "Insisting that all police officers carry guns will keep them safer on the streets."

4) Here are some points you could put in your **answer**:

The claim is reasonable	The claim is not reasonable
• The police regularly have to deal with armed criminals.	• Police officers could use alternatives — eg. stun guns.
• Guns would allow police officers to defend themselves more effectively against these armed criminals.	• Criminals who didn't carry guns before might start to arm themselves.
• It may discourage criminals from carrying guns.	• Criminals may be more likely to shoot armed police.

5) Your answer should **end** with a **conclusion** saying how **reasonable** the claim is — e.g.:

> Therefore, this claim is not very reasonable. Insisting that all police officers carry guns will not keep them safer on the streets.

Some questions will ask you to *Decide* which claim is the *Most Plausible*

1) In the exam you'll have to look at **both** sides of the argument and say which side is **most** plausible.

2) You'll also have to **explain** the **reasons** behind your decision.

> This question's still asking about the **same** document, but the **question** itself is **different** — it's asking about the **public's safety**. Always make sure you **read** the question **carefully**.

> Q2 Make a judgement on the relative plausibility (likelihood) of both outcomes (that the risk to the public will increase or decrease if all police officers carry guns.)

The risk to the public will increase

 This outcome is plausible
- Bystanders could be shot by mistake during a shootout, or an innocent person could be mistaken for a criminal and shot.
- The police already have alternatives to guns (e.g. stun guns, CS spray) which are safer.

This outcome is implausible
- All police who carry guns would get specialist training to minimise the risk to the public.

The risk to the public will decrease

 This outcome is plausible
- Police carrying guns can protect members of the public in situations where criminals are armed.
- Some criminals will be put off carrying weapons if the police are armed.

This outcome is implausible
- Some criminals might start carrying guns to fight back against armed police.

3) Then you have to **decide** which is the **most plausible outcome** based on these points.

4) You can argue **either way** — but **back up** your answer by saying **why** you think it's the **more plausible outcome**.

Assessing Credibility

Some questions will ask you to Decide which source is the Most Credible

1) Earlier in this section you looked at seven **different** credibility criteria which can **all** be useful in **judging credibility**.

2) You won't use them **all** at the **same time**, though — you'll need to **decide** which are the most **relevant** criteria for judging **each** source.

3) Criteria can be **used together** to help you decide how **credible** a source is.

You might be asked to assess the credibility of a document, its author, a claim or a person mentioned in the document — make sure your answer refers to the right thing.

Criteria which increase credibility	Criteria which decrease credibility
• Good reputation	• Bad reputation
• Good ability to see or perceive	• Lack of ability to see or perceive
• Neutrality	• Bias or vested interest
• Corroboration / consistency	• Inconsistency / conflict with other sources
• Relevant expertise / experience	• Lack of relevant expertise / experience

Some combinations of criteria give us a Strong reason to Believe a Source

The more **criteria** you have that **increase credibility**, the **more** credible your source is.

This source is **independent**, which means he has no **links** to either side of the debate. He is **neutral**.

An independent business consultant has agreed with the council that the area near the Craftfield Estate is the best position for the new factory: "Other factory developments I've seen in similar locations have been very successful in the past. This development will bring investment and hundreds of jobs to the town, so the advantages to the people living on the Craftfield Estate will outweigh the disadvantages of building the factory in this location."

He's also an **expert**. He has **expertise** in business matters, and **experience** of other, similar developments.

The two criteria of **neutrality** and **experience / expertise** combine together to **strengthen** this source's credibility. If we are told that the consultant **also** has a good **reputation** (for example if he's known to have made a number of **sensible** recommendations in the **past**), this would **increase** his credibility even **more**.

Some combinations of criteria give us a Strong reason to Doubt a Source

The more **criteria** you have that **decrease credibility**, the **less** credible your source is.

Mrs. Green has a **vested interest** in blocking the plans — she will **lose** money if the factory is built, so she has a **motive** for exaggerating its possible negative effects.

Mrs. Green lives on the edge of the Craftfield Estate, closest to where the factory will be built. She's strongly against the proposals, arguing that, "The factory will be very ugly and noisy — having it that close to my house will reduce its value and make it really difficult to sell. I doubt it'll bring much to the area — maybe a few jobs but that certainly doesn't outweigh the negative effect it'll have on us."

Mrs. Green might think this because she hasn't seen the plans for the factory — she may not have the **ability to perceive** all the evidence.

Mrs. Green has a **vested interest** and a **low ability** to see and perceive — these **combine** to **weaken** her credibility.

Use the word CRAVEN to help you remember the Credibility Criteria

It can be tricky keeping track of all those **criteria** — but remembering the word **CRAVEN** might help:

Corroboration / consistency	Reputation	Ability to see or perceive	Vested interest / bias	Experience / expertise	Neutrality

Assessing Credibility

You've got to make Decisions based on Relative Credibility

1) In the exam you'll be given a **document** containing **two sides** of an argument.

2) The **question** might ask you to make a **decision** based on **relative credibility** (see p.21) — you'll need to use **credibility criteria** to do this.

The Independent Group of Toy Safety Experts (IGTSE) has investigated the bestselling 'Zap-n-Jump' toy after concerns were raised by medical staff over its safety. Sandra Bellfour, an experienced nurse said, "I treat kids almost every day who claim to have been injured by this toy at home. It should be taken out of the shops immediately." Toy Days Ltd., who made the toy, has defended the 'Zap-n-Jump', saying, "It has been tested extensively and we have not identified any safety problems. Of course we will look into the toy's safety as concerns have been raised, but we are confident that it is perfectly harmless as we have a long and outstanding record of producing safe, exciting toys. It should remain on sale." IGTSE released this statement about its investigation: "We understand the concerns over the 'Zap-n-Jump' toy, and have performed a number of tests on it as part of our investigation. In our report for the government, we have concluded that while it does not break safety regulations for toys of this kind, it does carry a small degree of risk to children. We recommend that the toy should be withdrawn from sale."

Q1(a)   Come to a judgement as to whether the Zap-and-Jump toy will be removed from shops. You should make a reasoned case with a judgement based on the relative credibility of the two sides.

Start by assessing each Person or Organisation's credibility

1) You **won't** have to use **all** the credibility criteria when answering **questions** like this — some are more **relevant** than others and it'll usually be **clear** from reading the **document** which ones it would be best to **apply**.

2) When you've **decided** which credibility criteria to **apply**, make sure you explain **how** they affect **each** source's **credibility** — you'll miss out on **loads** of marks if you **don't** do this.

3) Here are some **examples** of what you **could** say:

Toy Days Ltd.

- Toy Days Ltd. has an "outstanding record of producing safe, exciting toys" which indicates that they have a **good reputation**. This **increases** the credibility of their **claim**.
- They have a "long" record of making toys so we can assume they're **experts**. This **increases** the credibility of their claim.
- But, they sell the toy to make a profit so they have a **vested interest** in keeping the toy in the shops. If they believe that the toy only poses a **very small risk**, it may lead them to **deny** that the toy is dangerous. This **decreases** the credibility of their claim.

IGTSE

- The IGTSE is **neutral** — we can tell this from the word "Independent" in its name. It has no links to Toy Days Ltd., or to any other toy companies. This **increases** the credibility of its **claim**.
- The IGTSE has lots of **relevant experience** and **expertise** as a professional toy safety group. It writes reports "for the government", which shows its opinion is well respected. This **increases** the credibility of its claim.
- As a professional body, the IGTSE has a **vested interest** in maintaining a good **reputation**. This **increases** the credibility of its claim.

Sandra Bellfour

- Sandra Bellfour treats children in hospital so she hasn't actually seen the fault in the toy. She has **poor ability to see or perceive** the evidence. This **decreases** the credibility of her claim.
- As an "experienced nurse", she is **neutral** — she has no reason to be biased towards either side. This **increases** the credibility of her claim.

4) Remember you're making your **judgement** based on **relative** credibility — **keep** your answer **focused** on comparing the credibility of the two sides.

5) To get **full** marks you've got to talk about the credibility of the people or organisations on **both sides** of the argument.

6) In this case, you'd **probably** decide that the **IGTSE** is the **most** credible source because **all** the criteria used **increase** its credibility — it's **neutral**, and it has **expertise** and a good **reputation**. We can confidently **believe** its claim.

7) Toy Days Ltd. **isn't** very **credible** because its **vested interest** gives it quite a strong motive to lie. Sandra Bellfour **isn't** very **credible** because of her **poor ability to see or perceive**, even though she is **neutral**.

Assessing Credibility

Now you have to predict *What Will Happen*

1) You now have to **decide** whether you think the toy will be **removed** from the shops **or not**.

2) Use the **credibility** of each source to help you make this **decision**.

Sandra Bellfour	IGTSE	Toy days Ltd.
1) Wants the toy withdrawn.	1) Wants the toy withdrawn.	1) Wants the toy to stay on sale.
2) Not very credible.	2) Very credible.	2) Not very credible.

3) The **most credible** source (IGTSE) recommends that the toy **should** be taken out of the shops.
The **only** source who wants the toy to stay on sale is **not** very **credible** (Toy Days Ltd.)

4) So the toy will **probably** be **removed** from the shops.

Sometimes you need *Extra Information* to judge credibility properly

1) In the exam you might be asked what **extra information** you need to judge a source's credibility.

2) The information you need will **depend** on the **criteria** you've used, e.g. if you've said that the source has **expertise**, you need to **know** what **qualifications** they have.

3) Here's an **example** of an exam question you might get:

> Q1(b)   Explain what extra information you need to reach one of your points of assessment in Q1(a) about the credibility of Toy Days Ltd. You should make one precise point.

Make sure your answer refers back to one of the credibility criteria you've used in Q1(a). If you refer to one you haven't mentioned in Q1(a), you won't get full marks.

4) **'Your points of assessment'** just means the **judgements** you made about Toy Days Ltd.'s **credibility** in Q1(a).

5) The question asks for **one point** so you'll **only** need to talk about vested interest, **or** reputation, **or** expertise, not all three.

6) Here are some **examples** of what you **could** say about each **criterion**:

The company says it has a good **reputation** for making safe toys.	We need more information about their **track record** to know whether their toys are **usually** safe.
They have a **vested interest** in the toy staying on sale as they'd **lose money** if it was removed from shops.	We need to know whether the company would be prepared to possibly **compromise safety** in order to make **more sales**.
They have **expertise** in toymaking — they've been doing it for a long time.	We need to know **how long** they've been making toys.

Practice Questions

Q1   Read the document on p.71 on dangerous dogs. Assess the plausibility of the following claim:
"The government should introduce a compulsory dog licence scheme."

Q2   What other information do you need about Sandra Bellfour to assess her credibility?

Exam Question

Q1   Read the documents on p.66-67. Look at Document 2 and assess the credibility of one claim from Jonathan Leadbeater and one from Mrs. Whittal. Use two credibility criteria in your assessment and explain how each strengthens or weakens the credibility of these claims.   [7 marks]

Predicting the outcome of an invisibility contest — there's nothing to it...

We've finally reached the end of the roller coaster ride that is credibility. We've been through good times and tough times during this section, but all things eventually come to an end. Take the happy memories of credibility criteria with you into the next section, and look back on this achievement with a smile on your face as you walk off into the sunset. Oh, and don't forget CRAVEN.

Intermediate Conclusions

Analysing arguments means being able to recognise all the different parts of the argument, knowing the technical terms for them and understanding what role they play. It's pretty important, so we thought it deserved its very own section...

The **Intermediate** conclusion **Supports** the **Main** conclusion

1) Some arguments have one or more **intermediate conclusions** as well as a **main conclusion**.
2) The intermediate conclusion gives **support** to the **main conclusion**, so it acts as a **reason**.
3) But it's also a **conclusion** because it is **supported** by **other reasons** in the argument.
4) Here's an **example** of an argument that contains an **intermediate conclusion**:

See p.4 if you need a reminder on main conclusions.

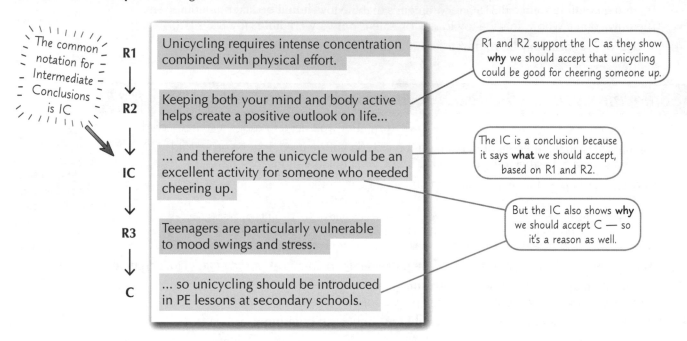

The common notation for Intermediate Conclusions is IC

R1
↓
R2
↓
IC
↓
R3
↓
C

R1 — Unicycling requires intense concentration combined with physical effort.

R2 — Keeping both your mind and body active helps create a positive outlook on life...

IC — ... and therefore the unicycle would be an excellent activity for someone who needed cheering up.

R3 — Teenagers are particularly vulnerable to mood swings and stress.

C — ... so unicycling should be introduced in PE lessons at secondary schools.

R1 and R2 support the IC as they show **why** we should accept that unicycling could be good for cheering someone up.

The IC is a conclusion because it says **what** we should accept, based on R1 and R2.

But the IC also shows **why** we should accept C — so it's a reason as well.

Here's **How** you **Identify** the **Intermediate Conclusion** in an **Argument**

1) **Identify all** the conclusions in the argument by looking for **indicator words** (p.6) and using the '**Therefore Test**' (p.7).
2) Put '**therefore**' in front of one conclusion and '**because**' in front of any other conclusion to see if it **makes sense** to use one conclusion as a **reason** to **support** the other. If it doesn't, **switch** them round and see if it **works** that way.
3) An **intermediate** conclusion will almost always be a **reason to accept** the **main** conclusion.

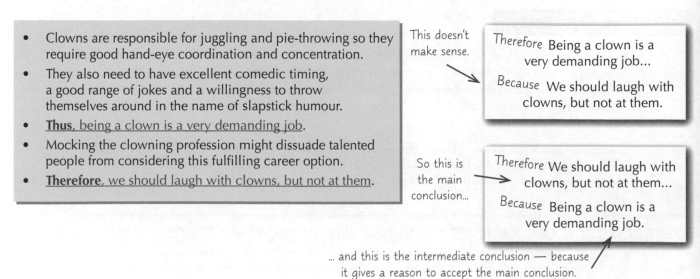

- Clowns are responsible for juggling and pie-throwing so they require good hand-eye coordination and concentration.
- They also need to have excellent comedic timing, a good range of jokes and a willingness to throw themselves around in the name of slapstick humour.
- **Thus**, being a clown is a very demanding job.
- Mocking the clowning profession might dissuade talented people from considering this fulfilling career option.
- **Therefore**, we should laugh with clowns, but not at them.

This doesn't make sense.

Therefore Being a clown is a very demanding job...

Because We should laugh with clowns, but not at them.

So this is the main conclusion...

Therefore We should laugh with clowns, but not at them...

Because Being a clown is a very demanding job.

... and this is the intermediate conclusion — because it gives a reason to accept the main conclusion.

Intermediate Conclusions

There are **Three** kinds of **Questions** about **Intermediate Conclusions**

1) The exam for **Unit 2** is split into **three sections**. **Sections A** and **B** will ask questions about **sources** like this:

> Source (i)
>
> Circus audiences have declined in number, and circuses with lion-taming acts have been particularly badly affected. Lion tamers still stick with tired old clichés, like whips and chairs, but these are too well-known to excite the audience. Therefore, lion tamers need to update their repertoire. Flamboyant song and dance is very popular nowadays, and would be dramatic and entertaining in a circus tent. Lion tamers should learn to tame lions with elaborate dance routines and rousing musical numbers.

2) **Section A** is made up of **multiple choice** questions, e.g.

> Read the argument above. Which of the following is an intermediate conclusion of the argument?
>
> a) Lion tamers should learn to tame lions with elaborate dance routines and rousing musical numbers.
>
> b) Lion tamers' acts are too well known to excite the audience.
>
> c) Numbers in circus audiences have declined.
>
> d) Lion tamers need to update their repertoire.

Either the question will give you the correct name and ask you to find the statement...

...or it will give you the statement and ask you to give the correct name.

> Read the argument above. What is the name given to the following element: "Therefore, lion tamers need to update their repertoire."
>
> a) Main conclusion
>
> b) Restricting the options
>
> c) Intermediate conclusion
>
> d) Hypothetical reasoning

3) In **section B**, you'll be given a passage like the one above and asked questions like these:

> Read the passage in the Resource Booklet. State an intermediate conclusion given in the passage.

> Read the passage in the Resource Booklet. The third sentence in the argument states: "Therefore, lion tamers need to update their repertoire." Name the argument element.

4) In **section C**, you'll have to **write your own** argument that includes an intermediate conclusion (see p.62).

Practice Questions

Q1 Complete this sentence: "In an argument, the intermediate conclusion _____"

a) supports the main conclusion but is also supported itself by reasons.
b) is always found in the middle of an argument.
c) is an example that supports the main conclusion.

Q2 What method should you use to check if a conclusion in an argument is the main conclusion or an intermediate one?

Exam Question

Q1 Read the paragraph below and state the intermediate conclusion of the argument. [3 marks]

"The possibility of killing someone who is innocent and has been wrongly convicted is appalling but inevitable, so the death penalty should be banned. Killing anyone, whether they're innocent or not, results in crippling guilt and therefore we should also consider the negative effects on the executioner."

Intermediate Conclusions — they'll be therefore you, when the rain starts to fall

Knowing how to tell the difference between a main conclusion and an intermediate conclusion is pretty important. After all, if you missed the main conclusion then you'd miss the whole point of the argument. That'd be a bit daft, so I'd recommend getting loads of practice. Oh, and remember that arguments can have more than one intermediate conclusion — especially long arguments.

Language for Analysis

There's a lot of words and definitions on these pages, which is bad. But learning them now will make everything later on easier to understand, which is good. Swings and roundabouts, as Florence and Dougal would say...

Critical Thinking uses a lot of Technical Terms

Critical Thinking uses a lot of different terms to describe what's going on in an argument. Being able to understand these terms is essential for understanding Critical Thinking, and being able to use them will impress the examiner. Grapple them into submission now, and later on it'll be plain sailing...

Ambiguous — If a statement is **ambiguous** then it has **more than one** possible **meaning**; e.g. *"You shouldn't approve of drug use on television"* could mean *"Don't say on television that you approve of drugs"* **or** *"You should disapprove of the television showing people using drugs."*

Assess — **Assessing** an argument means looking at its **strengths** and **weaknesses** and deciding if it's **effective**.

Belief — A **belief** is something that someone **thinks** is **true**. A belief can be true or false — it's not always possible to **prove** which.

Challenge — A **challenge** is a **question** that highlights a possible **weakness** in an argument. However, just because something can be challenged doesn't mean it's definitely a weakness — there might be a **reason** for it:
"Why doesn't your argument consider the results of the 1991 census?" asked Bob.
"Because those results are out of date now," answered Jim.

Coherent — A **coherent** argument **makes sense**, i.e. it's **logical** and **not confusing**.

Consistent — An argument is **consistent** if all the reasons can be **true at the same time**. If an argument is consistent it doesn't mean that all the reasons **are** true, just that it's **possible** for them all to be: *"Gavin is a lovely man, and a good dancer. But Ann is the best dancer, so she should be hired for the dance troupe."*

Contradict — Two statements **contradict** each other if they are the **exact opposite** of each other: *"The Prime Minister was a reliable and trustworthy man. However, he was unreliable and you couldn't trust him."* **Contradictions** are a very obvious type of **inconsistency** — they can't both be true at the same time.

Converse — The **converse** is a statement that **reverses** the two events in a statement of hypothetical reasoning. The converse of *"If it's not broken then don't repair it"* is *"If you don't repair it then it's not broken"*.

Counter — If you **counter** an argument then you **disagree** with it by providing a **claim** that **goes against** it: *"I disagree with your argument for a ban on fancy dress, because fancy dress is a chance to be creative."*

Imply — If an **unstated** claim **logically follows** from the meaning of a statement, then the statement **implies** that unstated claim. E.g. *"The sky is very overcast, so I won't need sunglasses"* **implies** that the sun is not visible and *"It's too sunny to go to the cinema and sit inside"* **implies** that it's better to do something outside when it's sunny.

Inconsistent — An argument is **inconsistent** if it contains two statements that **can't both be true** at the same time: *"Gavin is the worst dancer, and an awful person. However, Gavin is not as bad a dancer as Ann, so Ann should be fired from the dance troupe instead of Gavin."* This is inconsistent — it's impossible for Gavin to be the worst and also not as bad as Ann.

Language for Analysis

| Infer | To **infer** means to look at **reasons** or **evidence** and decide what **conclusions** they could support. |

| Knowledge | **Knowledge** is being **certain** of what is **true** because you have enough **information** to prove it. Liz might say *"I know the food will be spicy"*, and she can **prove** this because she cooked it and put lots of spices in it. Liz's friends might say *"I know the food will be spicy"* because Liz's food has always been spicy before, but they can't be **certain** it will be again. In this situation, Liz has knowledge, but her friends don't. |

| Opinion | An **opinion** is a **personal belief** that is based on **taste** or **preference**, not on facts: *"In Neil's opinion, it's better to save money because he prefers to feel reassured about the future. But in Terry's opinion, it's better to spend the money on things you want now because he prefers to enjoy life in the present"*. Opinions are neither **right** nor **wrong** — they're just a particular person's viewpoint. |

| Reasoning | **Reasoning** is the process of **drawing** a **conclusion** from **reasons** and **evidence**. For example, you might tell someone you didn't understand their reasoning if you didn't understand how they'd reached a certain conclusion. |

| Refute | To **refute** a claim means giving reasons which prove that it's wrong: *"I refute that claim because it's based on an out-of-date study"*. |

| Repudiate | If you **repudiate** a claim, you say that it's wrong but don't give any reasons why: *"I repudiate that, it's obviously wrong"*. |

| Strengths and Weaknesses | **Strengths** are the parts of an argument that help support the conclusion effectively. **Weaknesses** are parts that don't support the conclusion, or things missing from the argument that should be included. |

| Structure | The **structure** of an argument is the order that the reasons, conclusion and other parts are in. |

| Support | **Supporting** something means backing it up by giving reasons to accept it. |

Practice Questions

Q1 What is the correct term for the statement "Although your argument seems convincing, it is based on biased evidence so I can't accept your conclusion"?

  a) a refutation   b) a challenge   c) a repudiation   d) an opinion

Q2 What is the difference between these two statements?
"I know the bread is off because I've looked at it and it's covered in mould."
"I know the bread is off because it is past its sell-by-date."

Q3 What is the implication of the statement "the president has been assassinated"?

  a) The president is dead   b) The vice president is now in charge   c) Someone shot the president.

Exam Question

Q1 Read the paragraph below and state one inconsistency in the reasoning. [3 marks]
"Having children is a bad idea. Parents have to be selfless — you can't spend money on luxuries if there are nappies to buy and mouths to feed, and you can't have a lie-in if there's a screaming toddler to comfort. Also, it is selfish to have children — it increases the population of an overcrowded planet just because you want to pass on your genes."

I hate critical thinking — it's really got it infer me...

There's not much to say about this page — except "Eek, more definitions than I can shake a stick at. Abandon ship." But if you don't understand these words, studying Critical Thinking will be like wading through a treacle maze — slow, confusing, and you'll end up in a very dark place. If you do learn them, Critical Thinking will become a fluffy candy floss pillow of joy... maybe...

Drawing Conclusions

Drawing a conclusion is tricky — there's no foolproof, step-by-step method to getting it right. What's vital is that you think it through and use a bit of common sense. Practice makes perfect, so don't skip the questions on the next page.

Drawing a Conclusion means Deciding what Conclusion Follows from the Reasons

1) 'Drawing a conclusion' is just examiner-speak for looking at the **evidence** and **reasons** given and **deciding** what **overall point** they're making.

2) However, a set of reasons may have **more than one** possible conclusion. For example:

> Molly needs to improve her confidence and she would also like a way to meet people. She is quite musical and is good at physical, practical things like sport.

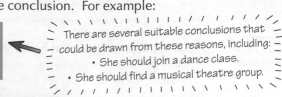

There are several suitable conclusions that could be drawn from these reasons, including:
- She should join a dance class.
- She should find a musical theatre group.

You might have to Identify the correct Conclusion

1) In the exam, you could get a **multiple-choice** question asking you to **choose** the **best conclusion** for a passage.

2) Look at the options and decide which is **supported** by **all** of the **reasons** and doesn't **rely** on anything **outside** of the reasons given. E.g.

> Learning a language allows you to communicate with more people and is really useful for going on holiday. Unfortunately, in the UK, foreign language lessons are only taught in secondary schools. They're not popular at all, as most teenagers find the lessons boring, frustrating and easily forgotten. If students already had a strong basic grasp of a language, the lessons would be more advanced and the topics would be more interesting.
>
> A child's brain grasps linguistic information with more ease than a teenager's. Also, at primary level lessons are more focussed on fun and games, so if languages were taught in primary schools the lessons would be less likely to be boring. However, children's brains develop very quickly and the new language would be forgotten if it wasn't developed and built on.

Read the argument. Which of the following is the conclusion that can best be drawn from the passage?

a) Secondary school language lessons need to be more fun.

b) Foreign language lessons should be moved off the secondary curriculum and onto the curriculum for primary schools.

c) Learning a language is too difficult for teenagers.

d) Foreign language lessons should also be put onto the primary curriculum.

This only considers the reasons in the first paragraph.

The reasons give support to improving lessons in secondary school, not abolishing them.

This isn't supported by any of the reasons.

This draws together all of the reasons.

You might have to Assess a Possible Conclusion

1) You could be given a **possible** conclusion and asked to **explain** if it could be **drawn** from the **reasons given**. E.g.

> Mary read the following passage and concluded that advertising doesn't need to be restricted in any way. Explain whether or not this can be concluded from the reasons given. [2 marks]

> Some people argue that advertising is dangerous and should be banned altogether, and it's true that it's partly responsible for society's distorted views on beauty. However, it does give consumers necessary information about a variety of products — which helps us make better decisions and get the best deal. It's also a vital part of business, and without it the economy would suffer.

2) Read the passage and ask yourself:

- Does the conclusion rely on something **not included** in the reasons?
- Does the conclusion **ignore** one of the reasons?
- Is the conclusion **supported** by **all** the reasons?

3) Here's a sample answer:

> It cannot be concluded from these reasons that advertising doesn't need to be restricted in any way, because that conclusion doesn't take into consideration the reason stated that advertising is "partly responsible for society's distorted views on beauty". This reason suggests that advertising does need some restrictions, but it doesn't need to be banned altogether.

Analogies

An *Analogy* is used to *Compare* one *Thing* to *Another*

1) **Analogies** work by **persuading** us that if we accept a **claim** about **one** of the things being **compared**, we will automatically accept the **same claim** about the **other** thing in the comparison. The reasoning in an analogy follows these **three steps**:

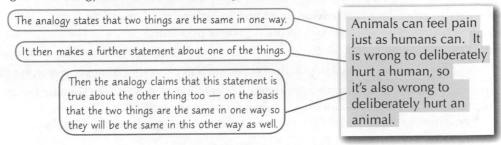

The analogy states that two things are the same in one way.

It then makes a further statement about one of the things.

Then the analogy claims that this statement is true about the other thing too — on the basis that the two things are the same in one way so they will be the same in this other way as well.

Animals can feel pain just as humans can. It is wrong to deliberately hurt a human, so it's also wrong to deliberately hurt an animal.

2) Sometimes the **reasoning** in an **analogy** isn't set out very **clearly**. For example:

It's ridiculous that gas companies are allowed to charge using estimated bills. It's as if the supermarket cashier could guess the total cost from just looking at your trolley, and that obviously wouldn't work.

3) To make it **easier** to work out what's **going on** in a **complicated** analogy, break it down into these **points**:

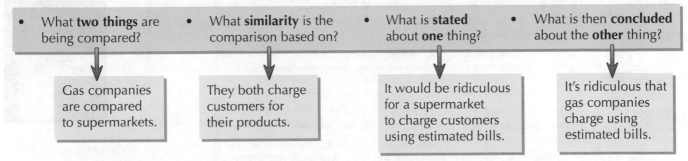

- What **two things** are being compared?
- What **similarity** is the comparison based on?
- What is **stated** about **one** thing?
- What is then **concluded** about the **other** thing?

Gas companies are compared to supermarkets.

They both charge customers for their products.

It would be ridiculous for a supermarket to charge customers using estimated bills.

It's ridiculous that gas companies charge using estimated bills.

4) **Indicator phrases** that might help you spot an **analogy** include: **"just like"**, **"as if"**, **"similar to"**.

5) But **not all** analogies use indicator words. Keep a look out for a **fact** about **one thing** being used to **support a claim** about **another thing** — based on a **similarity** between the two.

Practice Questions

Q1   What are you doing when you 'draw a conclusion'?

Q2   Decide what is being compared to freedom of speech in this analogy: "Freedom of speech is a human right, but you shouldn't use words to hurt people. After all, being licensed to own a gun doesn't give you the right to shoot at people."

   a) violence   b) human rights   c) being allowed to own a gun.

Exam Question

Q1   Explain whether the conclusion "Pasta sauce companies should lower their prices" can be drawn from the passage below.

   "A lot of families need evening meals that are cheap to buy and quick to make. Pasta sauces are a quick, easy way to make a meal. Shop-bought pasta sauce is usually quite expensive. Pasta sauce is just tomatoes blended with herbs and spices. Tomatoes and herbs can both be home-grown, just for the price of a pack of seeds."

[2 marks]

I've got analogy to learning — revision makes me sneeze...

Analogies are like tiny owls in knitted bobble-hats — they look cute, but then you realise they don't actually work. Sometimes the similarity between two things isn't enough to support the conclusion that the two things will then be the same in another way. But don't worry about evaluating analogies just yet — that's on p.48. For now, focus on understanding what's what. Twit twoo...

General Principles

A broad claim about how we should behave — due to morals or common sense — is called a General Principle.

A General Principle is a Rule about how we Should Behave

1) **General principles** are **guidelines** or **rules** about **behaviour** that could be followed in **many situations**, e.g. "Never hit a child".

2) Don't **confuse** general principles with **advice** about how to act in a **particular** situation. "I should be more patient with my nephews" is **not** a **general principle**.

3) General principles are usually **moral** or **ethical**, e.g. "It is always wrong to deliberately harm someone".

4) However, they can also be **social**, **legal** or **practical rules**, such as "You should never run with scissors".

5) But general principles **don't** have to **apply** to **everyone**. Statements which refer to **specific** groups of people but are stated as **rules** to be followed in **many situations**, such as "It is the parents' responsibility to make sure their children get a good education" are still **general principles**.

General Principles can work as Reasons or Conclusions

1) In the **exam**, you might be given an argument and asked to **identify** the **general principle** in it, or you might be given a sentence and have to **decide** if it's a **principle** or a **different** argument element.

2) Because general principles can be **reasons** or **conclusions**, you can't spot them by the role they're playing in an argument.

Halfway through, Philip completely forgot what role he was playing.

> Here, the general principle acts as a **reason**.

The banks are to blame for the financial crisis of 2008, because it was their mistake to allow such reckless borrowing and spending. Everyone should take responsibility for their own mistakes. Therefore, the banks should take responsibility and apologise for the consequences of their actions.

> Here, the general principle acts as a **conclusion**.

Cars can kill or severely harm you, even if they're driving at 30 mph. Drivers are paying attention to the road and don't expect people to step out in front of them. So pedestrians should always be very aware of what's going on around them.

3) There are some **indicator words** to look out for. For example:

- Right   • Wrong   • Unfair   • Should   • Always   • Never

4) These words don't always indicate a **general principle** — e.g. 'should' also indicates **conclusions** and **specific advice**.

5) You should use the indicator words as a **guideline**, and then **check** that the statement is a **principle** by making sure it's giving **advice** on **how to act** that could be relevant in **many different** situations.

Think Carefully about what is Relevant to the Argument

You could also get a question like this:

> Children who are forced to eat vegetables grow up to eat less healthily than children whose parents make vegetables optional instead of compulsory. Therefore, relaxed attitudes at the dinner table are better than strict rules.

> Which of the following is a principle that would most strengthen the reasoning in this passage?
>
> a) Parents should never be strict.
> b) Vegetables are full of vitamins.
> c) It's not always important for children to be taught table manners.
> d) It's better to eat healthily than unhealthily.

It's important to **read through** each option and think about how it **relates** to the **conclusion**:

- b) and c) do **strengthen** the argument — but they aren't **principles**.
- a) is a **principle** — but it's not **precisely relevant** to the **reasoning** of the argument.
- d) is the correct answer — it is a **principle**, and it is also the most **relevant** to the other reasons given in the argument.

> Or you might be asked to **suggest** a principle that would support this argument. Give a principle that's relevant to the conclusion, but make sure it's general enough to be a principle.

Explanations & Arguments

Explanations and arguments are easily confused, because they both give reasons to support a final statement. You need to know how to tell the difference, otherwise you'll get all in a muddle when analysing arguments that contain explanations...

An **Explanation** makes something **Clear** or **Understandable**

Explanations try to **improve understanding** of something by describing **why** it is the way it is. For example:

Jo won't win a trophy this year because a goat ate all her tulips, so she doesn't have anything to enter in the competition.

*This explains why Jo won't win by describing the events that **caused** her to lose her tulips.*

Rectangular pupils increase the depth and range of peripheral vision. This is helpful in mountainous landscapes — and that is why goats have rectangular pupils.

*This explains why goats have rectangular pupils by describing the **evolutionary** benefits.*

My goat is afraid of the shed because it is cold, dark and full of unfamiliar smells.

*This explains why the shed is scary by describing its physical **qualities**.*

If you're asked what the **difference** is between an **argument** and an **explanation** you need to say something like: 'An argument tries to **persuade** the reader to accept that something's **true**. An explanation describes **why** something is true, because the reader accepts that it's true but might not fully **understand** it'. E.g.

See p.4 for more on arguments.

There's less than 10 hours of daylight on winter days and chickens need about 15 hours of light each day to lay eggs. But farmers still have to meet customer demand for eggs throughout the winter. Luckily, it doesn't have to be 15 hours of *natural* light, artificial light works too. This is why farmers install lamps in their chicken coops in winter.

*The **reasons** in the explanation are mostly the **same** as the reasons in the argument.*

*The **explanation** uses the reasons to **show why** farmers install lamps. The **argument** uses the reasons to **persuade** us that we **should** install lamps.*

There's nothing nicer than a boiled egg and toasted soldiers on a cold winter's day. But there's less than 10 hours of daylight on winter days and chickens need about 15 hours of light each day to lay eggs. Luckily, it doesn't have to be 15 hours of *natural* light, artificial light works too. So if you want eggs throughout the winter, you should install lamps in your chicken coop.

The **Reasons** in an **Argument** are sometimes **Supported** by **Explanations**

The author supports the reason with an explanation showing why donkeys are intelligent.

Donkeys have cuddly, fluffy ears and soft noses. They're herd animals with sociable personalities, and they make very protective 'guard dogs'. They're intelligent because they're from the desert, where galloping on sand was tiresome and mostly useless, so they had to concoct plans to escape danger rather than run away from it. Donkeys are easy to feed and don't wear shoes like horses, so they're quite low maintenance. If you want a wonderful but unusual pet, you should buy a donkey.

*This is a **reason** why a donkey would be a wonderful pet.*

Practice Questions

Q1   Which of the following is the correct definition of a general principle?
a) Something that is always true   b) A guideline about general behaviour   c) Advice for a specific situation.

Q2   Is this an explanation or an argument? Explain why.
"It makes sense that more satsumas are sold than oranges. They're seedless and easier to peel, but still rich in vitamin C."

Exam Question

Q1   a)   Identify one principle used in the argument below.   [3 marks]
b)   Give one reason in support of this general principle.   [3 marks]

"Young children don't realise that taking something without paying is stealing. Taking a lolly might not seem the end of the world, but stealing is always wrong, even if it's something cheap. Young children might not understand a verbal explanation, so the best way to teach them right from wrong is to punish them. If my child stole something, I would smack them."

CGP's General Principle — everyone deserves a hug and a cuppa at the end of a section

Breathe a sigh of relief, grab a biscuit and put your feet up. Here endeth Section 3. You should be able to recognise an explanation, analogy or general principle from 50 feet, draw conclusions with both hands tied behind your back, and speak the lingo like a pro. If you can't — put down the biscuit, get back on your feet and back to the beginning of the section. Sorry...

Assessing the Use of Evidence

Evidence is supposed to convince us that we should accept the reasons in an argument. However, often the evidence doesn't actually give us grounds to accept the reasons, because it has been used weakly. You have to be able to spot the strengths and weaknesses of how evidence has been used. Here's how to tackle it...

You'll need to **Explain Why** the **Use** of **Evidence** is **Strong** or **Weak**

1) In Section One, you learnt how to talk about whether or not evidence was **representative** and how to recognise any problems with the way it's been **collected**.

2) This section shows you how to spot the **strengths** and **weaknesses** in the way evidence **backs up** a particular claim or reason, so you can assess **how well** evidence has been **used**.

3) Then page 44 will look at how to **answer questions** that ask you to **assess** the **use** of **evidence**.

Strong Evidence is Relevant

1) In Critical Thinking, you can't say evidence is **relevant** just because it's about **the same topic** as the reason.

2) To be **relevant**, the **evidence** must be about **exactly the same thing** as the reason. This includes:

   • timescale   • group of people   • geographic area

   For example:

   > In 2005, Detroit police used undercover surveillance and informants to fight organised criminals, and reduced crime by 72%. This shows that the British government doesn't need to invest more money in police weaponry — guns are not the only way to tackle violent criminals.

3) This example has two **weaknesses**. Firstly, the evidence is about police from **Detroit**, but it's being used to support a claim about **British** police. We can't be sure that what worked in Detroit will work in Britain because British police might have different skills, or the criminals might respond differently — so it's **not precisely relevant**.

4) Another **weakness** is that the evidence is about **organised** criminals, but it's used to support a claim about **violent** criminals. Techniques for dealing with the mafia or other **organised** crime groups won't necessarily **apply** to individuals who commit armed robberies, muggings or other **violent** crimes.

5) But if the evidence is **relevant** to the **reason** in any way, this **strengthens** the argument's use of evidence. For example, the evidence shows that crime-fighting methods that don't involve weapons can work, and this is a **strength** because it gives **some support** to the **conclusion** that police don't always have to use guns.

There's not always **Enough Evidence** to **Support** the **Claim**

1) Evidence may be **relevant** to the reason, but **not enough** by **itself** to **fully support** it.

2) If the reason needs **more evidence** to be **supported**, then the given evidence is **insufficient**. E.g.

   > We know Cyprus will be a great place for a holiday — it gets 326 days of sun a year.

   ⟵ Lots of sun may be relevant to having a great holiday, but it's not enough on its own. We need evidence about other factors — e.g. standard of beaches and hotels.

3) When certain information is **withheld**, it is called **selective use of evidence**. E.g.

   Evidence that would weaken the conclusion has been withheld — such as the link between smoking and cancer, and the fact that an addiction to smoking increases stress in the long term. All of this evidence proves that cigarettes are actually very bad for your health. ⟶

   > Many smokers use cigarettes to relieve stress — and with good reason. A scientific analysis of tobacco found that it causes the brain to release hormones that make you feel more relaxed. Stress is bad for your health, so this proves that cigarettes are good for your health.

4) Selective use of evidence, or using **insufficient** evidence, is a weakness because the reason won't be **fully supported**. The evidence is used **strongly** if it contains all the information **needed** for us to **accept** that the reason's **true**.

Assessing the Use of Evidence

Averages are not always Representative of the Whole Group

1) There are three different types of **average** — the **mean**, the **median** and the **mode**.

2) You **don't** need to know how to **calculate** the different types of averages, you just have to be **aware** that averages only give a **rough idea** of the overall group — so as evidence they might not offer **strong support** to a reason. E.g.

> The mean is all the values added up, then divided by the number of results: 946 ÷ 11 = 86

> Kathryn is a driving instructor. For eleven of her pupils, the total hours of driving lessons needed before passing their test were:
> •48 •59 •64 •65 •66 •67 •80 •80 •104 •129 •184

> The median is the middle value when all the values are arranged in order — 67

> The mode is the value that occurs most often — 80

3) Depending on which **type** of average was used, the average time it took to learn to drive could be **67**, **80** or **86** hours.

4) None of these averages show that **one person** learnt in **48 hours**, whilst **another** took **184 hours**.

5) You might be **given** an **argument** like this: "Kathryn is an excellent instructor. The average time it takes her to teach someone to drive is 67 hours, so there's no need to budget for more than 80 hours' worth of lessons."

6) If you had to **assess** the **use of evidence** in that argument, you could **say** something like: "For some people, it will take a lot longer than 67 hours to learn to drive, while for others it could take much less time. Therefore for some people it would be necessary to budget for 80 hours or more of lessons, while others could expect to spend less."

You might have to Evaluate Evidence from a Graph

1) Sometimes an argument will use a **graph** or a **table** as **evidence** to support a reason.

2) **Evaluating** data from a **graph** is just the same as **evaluating** any other piece of **evidence** — you need to check if it's **relevant** and gives **enough information**.

3) So you'll need to pay **attention** to any **labels**, **numbers** and **dates** to make sure you understand **exactly** what the data is saying. If there's a **key**, make sure you understand that too.

4) For example, you might be given this **graph** to support the **claim**: "Drama is more popular with students than any of the other GCSE options, so the drama department should get a bigger proportion of the 2011 budget."

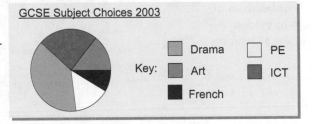

GCSE Subject Choices 2003

Key: Drama, PE, Art, ICT, French

5) There are **several reasons** why this claim might **not** be **true**. The **label** on the graph tells us that this pie chart only covers GCSE choices from **2003**, so we can't be sure that drama is still more popular in **2011**. The **key** shows us that drama is being **compared** to ICT, and the **ICT department** might need **more funding** than drama because ICT **equipment** is more **expensive**, even though **fewer pupils** might study it.

There are often Alternative Interpretations of Evidence

1) When an argument uses **evidence** to **support** a **claim**, that claim is just one **possible interpretation** of the evidence.

E.g.
> Newly qualified drivers aged 17 - 20 are twice as likely to have a crash as more experienced drivers. This shows that the practical driving test is too easy.

2) In this **example**, the author is claiming that the **reason** young drivers are more likely to crash is because the **driving test** is **too easy** and so they're allowed to drive without having enough **skills** or **experience**.

3) But there are lots of **other reasons** why young drivers might have more crashes. They might be **immature** and so more likely to take risks or they might drive more often at **night** when visibility is poorer.

4) If you can think of an **alternative explanation** for a piece of evidence then it **weakens** the author's **claim**.

Assessing the Use of Evidence

There are **Two Types** of Questions about **Evidence**

1) Multiple-choice questions might ask you to **decide** which **evidence** would most **strengthen** or **weaken** an argument:

> The average office worker spends 29 minutes of their working day making hot drinks. This is a waste of time, and tea and coffee runs cost employers thousands of pounds in lost work time. Tea should be banned in all workplaces to improve productivity.

This **most** weakens the argument, because it proves that tea breaks make workers more productive, so banning them wouldn't improve productivity.

This neither strengthens nor weakens the argument.

Q1   Which of the following pieces of evidence, if true, would most **weaken** the argument above?

 a) A five-minute break every hour boosts productivity, so it's more productive to take occasional rests than work flat out.
 b) Tea breaks are a sociable activity that boost happiness in the workplace.
 c) Office workers are more likely to daydream if they're drinking a hot drink.
 d) A cup of tea has 50 mg of caffeine, and a cup of coffee contains 100 mg.

This weakens the argument slightly, because it shows that tea breaks are positive, but doesn't challenge the main conclusion about loss of productivity.

This shows that hot drinks cause workers to lose concentration, so it strengthens the argument.

2) Other questions might ask you to **explain** one **strength** or **weakness** in the use of evidence:

> This argument says that office workers spend 29 minutes making hot drinks. Explain **one** strength or **one** weakness in the way this evidence is used to support the argument.   [3 marks]

The question might state the **evidence** and you'll have to identify which **claim** it is used to support, or it might state the **claim**, and you'll have to identify what **evidence** is used to support it.

> In this argument, the author claims that tea should be banned in all workplaces. Explain **one** strength or **one** weakness in the way the author has used evidence to support this claim.   [3 marks]

3) Usually there'll be **several** strengths or weaknesses, so there'll be **more than one** correct answer:

- It's important to **clearly state** what strength or weakness you've spotted, but that's **not enough** to get full marks.

  The evidence is weak because the survey only covers office workers.

  The evidence is strong because 29 minutes is a large proportion of the working day to spend on tea breaks.

- You must also give a developed **explanation** of how the **use of evidence** connects to the **reasoning**.

  The evidence is weak because it only covers office workers and cannot be applied more generally to all work environments such as hospitals or schools, so it doesn't support the claim that tea needs to be banned in all workplaces.

  The evidence is strong because 29 minutes is a large proportion of the working day to spend on non-work tasks, and this gives strong support to the claim that productivity would improve if people weren't allowed to make hot drinks.

Look at p.72 for another worked answer on explaining the use of evidence.

Practice Questions

Q1   Why is this evidence not relevant to the reason it's being used to support?

"Matthew Holt won the 'Most Inspiring' trophy in the Children's Literature Awards, and a range of stationery featuring his illustrations will soon be available to buy. This proves that he's one of Britain's most successful authors."

Q2   Give an alternative interpretation of the evidence given below:

"Studies show that children born to mothers who drank a lot of alcohol while pregnant are prone to violent, antisocial behaviour. This proves that consuming alcohol whilst pregnant will negatively affect the mental health of your baby."

Exam Question

Q1   How strongly do the results from the study support the main conclusion of the argument?   [3 marks]

"The average amount spent on university tuition will rise to £40,000 in the next 10 years. We surveyed two thousand 17-year-old sixth formers and 82% said this would cause them to have doubts about studying to degree level, and they would seriously consider alternative options. The cost of university is destroying many students' dreams of further education."

They nicked the 'ooligan who kicked my door in, cos 'e left loads of 'eavy dents

Well, I don't know about you, but one look at these pages has put me off ever using evidence ever again. It has to be exactly relevant and sufficient and not have any other explanations? Golly. It's a wonder anyone argues for anything any more. Luckily, it does mean that if you're asked to assess the use of evidence in the exam you'll have loads to say. Hurrah, a silver lining...

Identifying & Assessing Examples

Examples are a bit peculiar — they don't offer any logical support to reasons or conclusions. Instead, they illustrate reasons and make them seem stronger by grounding them in reality. So when you're evaluating 'em, don't forget that...

Examples can't **Support Conclusions** by Themselves

1) **Examples** show a **particular situation** where the **reason** is **true**, e.g.

> People often have different learning styles. My cousin Josh couldn't grasp the concept of evolution when it was explained to him verbally, but I drew a diagram and he got it right away. Teachers need to adapt to all the different styles if they want to be effective.

2) This illustrates the reason "People often have different learning styles" — but it's only one situation, so it's too **specific** to give logical **support** to the **conclusion** on its own.

3) Because they show that the reason has been **true** at least **once**, examples can make **reasons** more **convincing**. But they can't support conclusions by themselves.

Turn to p.13 for more on examples.

Vincent had illustrated his reasons beautifully — but it probably wouldn't help him pass his Critical Thinking exam.

You might be **Asked** to **Evaluate** an **Argument's** use of **Examples**

1) If you have to **evaluate** the use of an example, look at how the **example** is **connected** to the argument as a **whole**.

2) If it's **only** the example **supporting** the conclusion, then the example is being used in a **weak** way. E.g.

> Our bulldog is wonderful with children — he lets them pull his tail and play with him and is very patient with them. Clearly bulldogs are the perfect family dog.

This is weak because the example is only about one dog — so there's not enough reasons to accept a general conclusion about all bulldogs.

3) If the **conclusion** is **supported** by **reasons**, and the example is **illustrating** one of the reasons to make it more **convincing**, then the example's being used in a strong way. E.g.

> Not only do sports like football and rugby improve teamwork on-pitch, they also help social skills off-pitch. Our local junior teams always get together for juice and snacks after the match, as well as organising days out and trips away. If your child needs bringing out of their shell you should try signing them up to a sports team.

Here, the conclusion is supported by the reason and the example makes the reason more convincing — so it's a strong use of an example.

Examples also need to be **Relevant**

1) An example won't make a reason more **convincing** unless it's **relevant**. Examples are usually relevant if they're:

- About precisely **the same situation** as the reason — the same **timescale**, **area**, **group of people**, etc.
- **Typical** of the group being discussed — without any reason to think it might be an **exception** from the norm.

E.g.
> Exercising isn't a good way to lose weight. When Matt Hegarty was training for a marathon, he was exercising for at least 2 hours a day every day — and he put on weight.

The reason is about people wanting to lose weight, but Matt Hegarty was exercising as preparation for a marathon, not to lose weight. The aims are very different, so the example isn't relevant.

> Horror films often have serious effects on people's mental health. Last year, a young man attacked and murdered an innocent passer-by just hours after watching Screwdriver II at the cinema.

This example isn't relevant because it's an exception. One man's extreme actions aren't representative of the large group of people who watch horror films.

2) Sometimes it doesn't **matter** if examples are **exceptions**. In the following argument, the reason is only claiming that exercise isn't **always** good. In this case, it doesn't matter that the examples are exceptions because they still illustrate the reason's claim that **sometimes** sport can be bad for your health.

> Doing exercise isn't always good for you. Runners can damage their joints because it's a high impact sport, and snow-boarders frequently break bones. So always check with your doctor before starting a new exercise regime.

Assessing General Principles

As you saw on p.40, general principles are claims about how we should behave. When you're assessing a principle, you have to think about whether it's relevant to the argument, but also how many other situations it could be relevant to.

General Principles need to be Relevant to the Argument

For example:

> The government shouldn't allow people to inflict prolonged suffering on animals. Fox-hunting forces a living creature to run for its life, before being savagely killed. The hunt often takes hours, and causes the fox a lot of suffering. Therefore, banning fox-hunting is the right action to take.

No foxes were harmed during the making of this revision guide.

1) The **principle** is "The government shouldn't allow people to inflict prolonged suffering on animals" and the **conclusion** is "banning fox-hunting is the right action to take".

2) Not everyone would necessarily agree that foxes suffer during a fox-hunt. But the argument **provides reasons** to consider it prolonged suffering — so the **principle** is shown to be **relevant** to the **situation**.

3) This means the **principle supports** the **conclusion** that fox-hunting should be banned.

A Strong general principle applies in Many Situations

1) When **assessing** the use of **general principles** in arguments, you need to look at how **generally** the principle is **true** by thinking about how many **other situations** the principle **applies** in.

2) If the principle applies in a **lot** of situations then it's **strong**. But if there are many situations where it **doesn't apply** then it's a **weak** general principle. For example:

- "The government shouldn't allow people to inflict prolonged suffering on animals" **applies** in these situations:

A lot of people abuse their **domestic pets** by keeping them in unsanitary cages and starving them. The government shouldn't allow people to inflict prolonged suffering on animals, so these people should be punished.	The welfare of **farm animals** needs to be ensured — farmers might neglect or over-work their animals in an attempt to save money. The government shouldn't allow people to inflict prolonged suffering on animals, so farms should have to undergo routine inspections.	Exotic animals like elephants have many complex needs that can't be met if they're forced to travel constantly as part of a circus. The government shouldn't allow people to inflict prolonged suffering on animals, so something must be done to protect **exotic circus animals**.

3) So the **principle** seems to be a **strong** one, because it applies in so **many** situations.

Sometimes a Principle will Clash with Another Principle

1) A lot of people would argue that the **principle** about animal suffering **doesn't** give **strong support** to this argument:

> The government shouldn't allow people to inflict prolonged suffering on animals. **Medical research on animals** often involves dissection without anaesthetic, and other experiments that subject the animals to a great deal of suffering. Therefore, banning medical research that causes animals suffering is the right action to take.

2) If the government **banned** medical research on animals because it exposed animals to **suffering** then many humans would suffer instead. So it **clashes** with the **principle** "we must protect humans from disease and suffering".

3) If two principles **clash** with one another like this, you need to **decide** which is **stronger**. In this example, most people would probably agree that "we must protect humans from disease and suffering" is the **stronger principle**.

4) Although the animal-suffering principle is **relevant** to the medical research example and **applies** in many situations, it **doesn't** strongly **support** the **conclusion** to ban medical research because it **clashes** with a **stronger** principle.

5) "The government shouldn't allow people to inflict prolonged suffering on animals" gives **strong support** to the **fox-hunting example** — because it's **relevant**, **applies** in **many** situations and **doesn't clash** with a stronger principle.

6) However, if an argument uses a principle that's **irrelevant**, **doesn't apply** in many situations, or that **clashes** with a **more important** principle, then the principle would **not** give **strong support** to the **conclusion**.

Assessing Hypothetical Reasoning

Hypothetical reasoning looks at what might happen as a result of something else happening — it's usually in the form "if, then". Have a peek at p.9 if you need a quick reminder...

Hypothetical Reasoning can Strengthen or Weaken an argument

1) You might be **asked** to **evaluate** the use of **hypothetical reasoning** in an argument — which means you have to say if the hypothetical reasoning **strengthens** or **weakens** the argument, and **why**.

2) **Strong** hypothetical reasoning will be a **credible** claim that gives a **good reason** for accepting the **conclusion**.

3) **Weak** hypothetical reasoning will be a claim that's very **unlikely** or **unbelievable**, or **isn't relevant** to the conclusion.

4) So there are **four** things to consider when **assessing** if the **hypothetical reasoning** supports the argument:

- Is it **true** that one event (the **consequence**) will happen as a **result** of the other event (the **condition**)?

  If I explain that I had a date with my boyfriend, then my teacher won't mind that I haven't done my homework. Therefore I won't do my homework.

  The condition "explaining I had a date with my boyfriend" won't, in most cases, lead to the consequence "my teacher won't mind". So the hypothetical reasoning can't support the conclusion.

- Is the condition **possible** or **likely** to happen?

  If aliens invaded tomorrow, then no one would notice I hadn't done my homework. Therefore I won't do my homework.

  It's possible, but very unlikely, that aliens will invade. If the condition is questionable or unlikely, the hypothetical reasoning won't support the conclusion.

- Does the reasoning **support** the conclusion?

  If I'm really nice to my teacher then I might not get into trouble for not doing my homework. Therefore I don't need to do it.

  The reasoning is indefinite — it only claims that "I **might** not get into trouble". This doesn't support the **definite** conclusion "I don't need to do it".

- Does the claim offer **some support** to the conclusion, but need **more information** to **strengthen** that support?

  If I want to do well at school, then I need to change my homework habits. Therefore I should start going to Jenny's house when I have homework to do.

  This reasoning offers some support to the conclusion — but the argument needs more information to strengthen it. E.g. "Jenny is hard-working and will be a good influence".

Practice Questions

Q1 Think of two situations where each of the following principles wouldn't apply.
  a) It's important to respect other people's beliefs.   b) Everyone has the right to personal privacy.

Q2 How well do each of these examples of hypothetical reasoning support their conclusions?
  a) If you study critical thinking, then you might become a philosopher.
     But philosophers don't earn very much, so you should study economics instead.
  b) I'll lose my job if I take a sick day, so I should struggle into work.
  c) If I fall down the stairs, then I will definitely break my back, so it will be safer for my health to take the lift.

Exam Question

Q1 Explain one weakness in the use of examples in the following argument: [3 marks]

  "PE lessons shouldn't be compulsory in schools. I know someone who broke his leg during a break-time game of football with his friends, which just shows how dangerous sports can be in a school environment".

"Doctor, doctor, I've got to assess." — "Oh dear... which one do you sit on?"

I can't stress this enough — it's no use just saying 'this is weak hypothetical reasoning' or 'this general principle is wrong'. Explain WHY and HOW it affects the argument. That's very important. More important than remembering to hold on to your chocolate biscuit when you dunk it. Which is very very important — unless you enjoy scooping gooey blobs of regret out of your mug. <sob>

Evaluating the Use of Analogies

You met analogies earlier — they're where two things are shown to be similar, and that then supports a claim that they're similar in another way too. Evaluating them means deciding if the two things are similar enough to support the claim.

Identify Exactly what is Going On

1) Not all analogies **explicitly state** their **conclusion** or **explain each situation** clearly. Before you start to **evaluate** the analogy, make sure you know **exactly** what is happening:

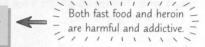

Fast food is addictive and can cause significant health problems, such as obesity, which might lead to low self-esteem and other social problems. You may as well give your child a hit of heroin along with their burger, chips and fizzy drink.

- What **two situations** are being **compared** in the analogy, and **what similarity** is the **comparison** based on?

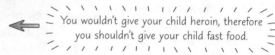

Both fast food and heroin are harmful and addictive.

- What **conclusion** is being drawn due to that **similarity**?

You wouldn't give your child heroin, therefore you shouldn't give your child fast food.

2) Once you understand the **basic structure** of the analogy, then you can begin to **evaluate** it. If you need more of a **detailed reminder** about what an analogy is, look back to page 39.

Weigh up the Similarities and Differences

1) To **evaluate** the use of **analogy** in an argument, you need to know if it's a **good comparison** of two situations. To do this you need to ask:

- Are there **significant similarities** between the **two situations** that are **relevant** to the conclusion?
- Are there any **important differences** that would affect whether we'd **accept** the **conclusion**?

2) If the analogy has **more important differences** than **similarities**, then it doesn't give **grounds to accept** the **conclusion**.

Heroin and fast food both cause addiction and health problems, which parents wouldn't want to their children to have.

Fast food is highly addictive and causes significant health problems, such as obesity, which can lead to low self-esteem and other social problems. You may as well give your child a hit of heroin along with their burger, chips and fizzy drink.

Heroin is illegal. Heroin also has more health risks — such as contaminated needles or overdose. The occasional burger can be balanced out by eating healthily the rest of the time, but just one shot of heroin is always a serious health risk.

3) Don't discuss **irrelevant** similarities and differences that don't **affect** the **conclusion**. E.g. "Fast food is packaged in bright colours, so it's appealing to consumers. Heroin is not nicely packaged, so children probably wouldn't want it". This difference is not **relevant** to the **conclusion** about fast food being **harmful**.

Link your Evaluation to the Argument's Reasoning

1) In the exam, make sure you **explain how** the analogy **links** to the argument's **conclusion** and **why** it's strong or weak.

In the following argument, the author uses an analogy about revision. Make **two** evaluative points about this analogy. [6 marks]

You wouldn't go running with someone who was slower, because you wouldn't reach your full potential. It's the same when you're revising. It might be nice to have company, but if the person you're revising with is less intelligent it might affect your final results.

In both running and revision you have to push yourself to improve, and a weaker companion would affect how motivated you felt to try your hardest. ✓

In running you have to push yourself to improve, and it's the same with revision.

2) The first answer is better — it **explains** how **the similarity links** to the **conclusion** about not achieving the best results.

3) If the question asks for **two** points of evaluation, make sure each point discusses a **different aspect** of the analogy — if the examiner thinks you're just **repeating** yourself then you might **miss out** on **marks**.

Offering Alternative Explanations

Some Arguments use Explanations to Support Conclusions

1) Remember, an **explanation** describes **why** something is the way it is, to help us **understand** it better.

2) They often **look like** arguments, because they give **reasons** that connect to a final **statement**.

3) The important **difference** is that explanations aren't trying to **persuade** us of anything. The final statement is already **accepted** as **true**. For example:

Turn back to p.41 if you need to know more about explanations.

> He got soaked because he forgot to check the weather forecast and didn't bring an umbrella. If he doesn't want it to happen again, he needs to be better prepared.

This statement is accepted as true...

... but it is explained with two reasons to show why it is true.

The explanation is then used to support a conclusion about how to avoid getting soaked again.

You might be Asked to Give an Alternative Explanation

If you have to think of an alternative explanation in the exam, make sure the explanation you give is **well developed** and **clearly different** from the explanation already given in the argument. E.g.

Q1 The following argument says that the U.K.'s debt problem has been caused by people's greed and impatience. Give an alternative explanation for this problem of debt. [2 marks]

Many people in the U.K. have debt problems. They can't control their greed, or wait patiently until they've saved enough money, so they buy what they can't afford. If we brought back the values of patience and self-restraint then the problem would solve itself.

- This doesn't **clearly explain** how expensive houses lead to debt.

  → Houses are too expensive. ✗

- This is a **good** explanation because it gives a **detailed description** of the chain of events that lead from high mortgages to debt.

  → U.K. banks allow their customers to have very high mortgages, which encourages people to take on a larger loan than they can realistically cope with. This means people get into more and more debt as they struggle to hold onto their homes.

This is just **one** possible alternative. There are loads of explanations you could have given and still got the marks — student loans, high interest rates, etc.

Practice Questions

Q1 What two things are being compared in this analogy?

"We don't blame the weather reporters for the bad weather — it's just their job to report what's going on. Why then is it okay to blame the newspapers and magazines for the decline in moral standards? They're just reporting the facts."

Q2 The following argument suggests that children are hyperactive after eating shop-bought sweets because of the E-numbers and artificial additives. Offer an alternative explanation for hyperactivity after eating sweets.

"Shop-bought sweets make children hyper, because of all the E-numbers and artificial additives used. Therefore, home-made cakes or biscuits would be a better way to give your child a treat but also keep them calm."

Exam Question

Q1 Make two points of evaluation about the analogy below. [6 marks]

"People who buy cheap, throwaway fashion are as guilty of exploiting people as the plantation owners who used to profit from slave labour. After all, the only reason clothes are so cheap is because the clothes factories keep their workers in appalling conditions and pay them barely enough to live on."

This page's like a penguin — black and white with a joke on the bottom...

Analogies and explanations are hard work — you have to put your thinking cap on and come up with loads of ideas about differences and similarities, or even alternatives. Hmph. They don't ask for much do they... On the bright side, at least you've still got time to get some practice at it, so you're less likely to eat your exam paper in an irrational panic on the day. Hurrah.

Flaws

So far we've looked at argument parts that can be strengths or weaknesses, depending on how they're used. Now we'll cover flaws — flaws are always weaknesses. You need to be able to recognise them and explain how they weaken an argument.

Flaws are Errors of Reasoning

1) A **flaw** is a **mistake** in the **reasoning** used to **link** an argument's **reasons** to its **conclusion**.

2) If an argument contains a flaw, it usually means we **can't accept** the **conclusion**.

3) An important thing to remember is that flaws **always weaken** an argument.

4) There are **fifteen** flaws you need to learn for the **exam**. They're all explained in detail on these next six pages.

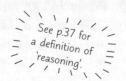
See p.37 for a definition of 'reasoning'.

The Conclusion might be about something Different to the Reasons

1) An **unrelated conclusion** happens when an argument's **reasons** and **conclusions** aren't **relevant** to one another.

2) It's not always obvious that the reasons **aren't related** to the conclusion — often they're both about the same **general topic** but not about precisely the **same aspect** of that topic.

This flaw is also known as "arguing from one thing to another".

3) In this example, both the **reasons** and the **conclusion** are about **education** — but the reasons are about an **exam-focused** system and are not related to the conclusion about **punctuation**:

> The education system today is entirely focused on how to pass exams. This means exams don't test the full breadth of a student's knowledge of a subject — only their knowledge of the specification and assessment objectives. It's no wonder so many A-level students don't know how to use an apostrophe correctly.

Conflation means using two Different words as if they mean Exactly the Same

1) Conflation often happens because two words have **very similar** meanings. But that doesn't make them **identical** — so saying something is true about one doesn't mean it will be true about the other. E.g.

We also looked at conflation on p.18.

> Mature people make better decisions. I'm older than you, so you should follow my decisions instead of your own.

Being mature is not the same as being older, so the reason and conclusion are about different things, and the conclusion is unsupported.

Max looked young, but he had a very mature attitude to life.

Some arguments Confuse Necessary and Sufficient Conditions

1) A **necessary** condition for something is one that **must happen** or **be true** for something else to happen, e.g.

> • To be a comedian it is necessary to be funny.

2) A **sufficient** condition for something is one that is **enough** for that something to happen, e.g.

> • She has a long history of violence against teachers and other pupils — this is sufficient reason to expel her.

3) If an argument **confuses necessary** and **sufficient** conditions then the reasoning is **flawed**. E.g.

> I am funny, therefore I'll definitely be a comedian, even though I'm terrified of public speaking.

You have to be funny to be a comedian, so being funny is a necessary condition. This argument claims that because it's necessary, it's also sufficient. But it's not sufficient because you need other qualities too — such as the ability to speak in public.

> I won't be expelled — even though I did deliberately burn down the science block — because I don't have a long history of violence against teachers and other pupils.

This example assumes that because a long history of violence is sufficient then it might be necessary as well. Although a history of violence will get you expelled, it's not necessary because you can get expelled for other things too.

Flaws

A **Slippery Slope** argues that one **Small Event** will lead to an **Extreme Result**

1) **Slippery slope** reasoning claims that **one small event** will cause an **extreme result** — but gives no **reason** to **accept** that the first **event** and the final **result** are **logically linked**.

> Even non-violent video games are a danger to your child. They start off peacefully racing cars round a track, avoiding banana skins. But before you know it, they haven't left their bedroom all day because they're addicted to the virtual thrill of shooting innocent bystanders whilst hurtling round a city in a stolen vehicle.

2) This reasoning is **flawed** because no **reason** is given to make us accept that playing a childish racing game will **lead** to an **addiction** to violent video games. The link between the **first event** and the **final result** is very weak.

In a **Circular Argument** the **Conclusion Repeats** one of the **Reasons**

1) In a **circular argument**, one of the **reasons** is saying basically the same thing as the **conclusion**.

2) Because the reason and conclusion are the **same**, there's nothing to **persuade** us to **believe** the conclusion, so we can't accept it. For example:

> It is fair to confiscate his phone because that is a just punishment. ⟵ 'Fair' and 'just' mean the same thing — so the reason just repeats what the conclusion said.

Begging the **Question** is a **Specific Type** of **Circular Argument**

1) If an argument is **begging the question**, it means you have to **already** **accept** the **conclusion** before you can **accept** the **reasons**. For example:

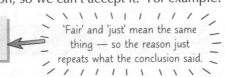

> You could only accept the reason 'everyone has the right to free speech' if you **already** believed the conclusion that it's **wrong** to silence people's opinions.

> Everyone has the right to free speech, therefore it's wrong to try to silence other people's opinions.

> The Bible says God is always right. We know the Bible is true because it is the word of God. Therefore, God is always right.

> To accept the reason "the Bible is true because it is the word of God" you must already accept the conclusion that "God is always right".

2) This is **flawed** reasoning because **accepting** the **conclusion** before **accepting** the **reasons** is the exact opposite of what is supposed to happen in an argument.

Practice Questions

Q1   "If voluntary euthanasia became legal, choosing death because you were disabled would become the norm, so the disabled who wanted to live would feel pressured not to become a burden to society. Before we knew it, the sanctity of life would be forgotten and doctors would start killing people without their permission."

a)   Name the flaw in the argument above.
(i) Conflation (ii) Unrelated conclusion (iii) Slippery slope (iv) Circular argument

b)   Explain why this flaw means the reasoning doesn't work.

For a guide on how to answer this kind of question look at p.55.

Exam Question

Q1   Name the flaw in the argument below and, referring specifically to the reasoning in the argument, explain why the argument does not work.   [3 marks]

"Chewing gum is unhealthy — most gum is sweetened with aspartame, and consumption of aspartame has been linked with cancer. So the council really must do something about the sticky blobs of gum littering our pavements."

And now for an unrelated conclusion...

Mrs Pheen's tips for a tip-top tea party: Lay the table with a fresh bunch of wild flowers, a plate of scones warm from the oven and little bowls of cream, butter and jam. Add a fat yellow teapot, a milk jug and a jumble of mismatched cups and saucers. Invite a mix of eccentric characters. Discuss politics or culture whilst wearing elaborate hats and sticking your little fingers out.

Flaws

These flaws are a jolly old laugh aren't they? Oh alright, maybe you're not rofl-ing right now — but you wait 'til you see a hasty straw person sweeping up some ad hominems. Then, my friend, you will laugh. Maybe even out loud.

Tu Quoque *flaws say "I'll* Do Something *because* Someone Else *does it* Too"

1) A **Tu Quoque** flaw **defends** an **action** by reasoning that the **same action** has been done by **others**:

> I don't think I need to reduce my personal carbon emissions by walking to the shops instead of driving. After all, the Chinese government aren't cutting the carbon emissions of their factories, so why should I cut mine?

> All my friends volunteer at charity shops, therefore I should too.

Their fashion statement was based on flawed reasoning.

2) The actions might be **immoral** or **harmful** or they might be **nice** — but it's **always** flawed to argue that you should do something **just** because someone else is doing it.

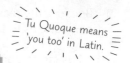

Tu Quoque means 'you too' in Latin.

'Two Wrongs *don't make a* Right' *is very* Similar *to* Tu Quoque

1) **Tu Quoque** argues that you can do something just because someone else has done the **same** thing. '**Two wrongs**' justifies a harmful action by saying that it's acceptable because other people have behaved badly in a **different** way:

> I vandalised the politician's garden, but he deserved it because he was corrupt.

The difference between 'Tu Quoque' and 'Two wrongs don't make a right' is quite subtle. If you're not sure which one is which in the exam both flaws can be described as "reasoning from wrong actions".

2) This is **flawed** because someone doing **something wrong** is **not a reason** for you to do **something else** that's **wrong**.

There are *Two Types* of Unwarranted Generalisations — Hasty *and* Sweeping

1) **Generalisations** use some **information** about **part** of a group to make **claims** about the **whole** of that group or **one individual** in it.

2) When an argument uses a **claim** about a **few** things to support a **conclusion** about **lots** of things or **everything** it's called **hasty generalisation**. For example:

> I've only met two librarians in my life, but they were both loud, arrogant and rude. Therefore, I try to avoid all librarians now.

3) It's flawed because the **conclusion** is based on **insufficient evidence**. A claim about two librarians is **too specific** to tell us anything **reliable** about all librarians.

4) **Sweeping generalisations** are the **opposite**. They use a **claim** about **many** things to support a conclusion about **one individual case**. E.g.

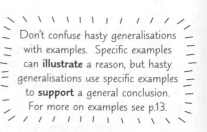

Don't confuse hasty generalisations with examples. Specific examples can **illustrate** a reason, but hasty generalisations use specific examples to **support** a general conclusion. For more on examples see p.13.

> A lot of rugby players are loud, arrogant and rude. I prefer reserved, polite people. Steve is a rugby player — therefore I won't like him.

5) But just because something is **often** true or **generally** the case, it isn't **sufficient evidence** to tell us anything **definite** about one **specific** case, so it's flawed.

6) You might be asked in the exam to **explain** why a generalisation is flawed. It **isn't enough** to say "This is flawed because Steve might be a quiet, polite rugby player." Instead, explain **why** it doesn't work: "A claim about many rugby players is used to support a conclusion about Steve. This doesn't work because Steve might be an exception and no evidence is given to suggest that he's not."

Flaws

The Straw Person Flaw Distorts the Counter-argument

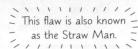
This flaw is also known as the Straw Man.

1) The **Straw Person** flaw occurs when an argument is **dismissing** a **counter-argument** (see p.8).
2) The **counter-argument** is **misrepresented** or **distorted** to make it **easier** to dismiss.

> Some people argue that it's best for young children if their mother stays at home, because mothers are instinctively nurturing. But it's clearly wrong to say that mothers are only good at cooking, cleaning and general domestic drudgery. Mothers have all sorts of skills, so they should be allowed to have a career if they want.

3) This **misrepresents** the argument for stay-at-home mothers — saying mothers are instinctively nurturing is **not** the **same** as saying they're only good at domestic drudgery.
4) By **distorting** the opposing view, or focusing on one **irrelevant** weak spot, the argument **misses the point** and attacks a counter argument that **doesn't exist** or doesn't really matter.

5) If you have to explain why something is a straw-person flaw, say something like: "The argument **misrepresents** the counter-argument, because the argument for stay-at-home mothers isn't claiming that mothers are only good at general domestic drudgery. This means the counter-argument hasn't been **properly dismissed** — so the argument is flawed".

Ad Hominem flaws Attack the Person arguing instead of the Argument

1) An **ad hominem flaw** is when an argument tries to dismiss a counter-argument by **attacking** the **person** arguing, rather than their argument.
2) The counter-argument could still be **strong** and **valid** in itself — it **doesn't matter** what the person making it is like.
3) This is why ad hominem reasoning is **flawed** — it **doesn't give** any **reason** to dismiss the counter-argument, e.g.

> Benefit application procedures are too strict. Lady Olivia James argues that we need the procedures to be really strict to make it harder to cheat the welfare system. But she's obviously just a rich snob who has no idea what it's like to struggle for money and rely on benefits for survival.

4) **Ad hominem** flaws can also be used to **persuade** you to **accept** an argument because the person arguing is **nice**:

> Nurses are caring, sensitive people, so their argument that hospitals needs more investment must be justified.

Practice Questions

Q1 Name the flaw in each of the following arguments:
   a) Christmas should always be spent with friends, not family. I can't stand my parents, and I know some people who feel the same. Clearly no one ever wants to spend time with their relatives.
   b) The theory of evolution argues that we share a few similar features with monkeys, so they must be our ancestors. But we share similar features with every mammal, and they can't all be our ancestors. Evolution is wrong.

Q2 Explain why Tu Quoque is flawed reasoning.

Exam Question

Q1 Name the flaw in the argument below and explain why the reasoning doesn't work. [3 marks]

"Some students argue that a rise in tuition fees is unfair and forces many people to miss out on higher education. But look at how they've protested against the rise — rioting in the streets and storming Parliament. We obviously don't need to pay any attention to the opinions of such out-of-control louts."

Tu Quoque — isn't that the band with Bono in?

That's funny, because Tu Quoque means "you too" in Latin— geddit? Ahem, moving on... How daft is Tu Quoque? If someone's pinched my cream bun I think it's perfectly logical to go and pinch someone else's. I need the sugary goodness to survive the day... mmm, cream buns... But enough about my lunchtime woes — as sensible as it might seem, it's just not thinking critically.

Flaws

Oh dear, yet more flaws, and some of these have confusing names too. Pay attention and make sure you don't write about Restricted Cause and Effect, Post Hoc options, or unicorn-riding leprechauns — because those things do not exist.

If an argument *Ignores* other *Possibilities* it's called *Restricting* the *Options*

1) An argument might try to present its **conclusion** as the **best option** by only discussing a **limited range** of choices. E.g.

> Vegetarians are difficult dinner party guests. Either you've got to go to the extra hassle of cooking a separate dish for them or disappoint the other guests by not serving meat. I've tried asking them to bring their own food — but they seem to find that insulting. I find the best option is just to not invite them.

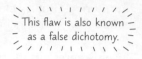
This flaw is also known as a false dichotomy.

2) This is flawed reasoning — if there are other more **appealing alternatives**, and the argument **doesn't mention** these alternatives or offers **no reason** to **dismiss** them, then you won't be **persuaded** to accept the **conclusion**.

3) A good way to show this is a flaw is to give the **possibilities** that the argument **ignores**. You could say something like "This argument is flawed because it restricts the options to cooking a separate dish for vegetarians, or disappointing other guests by not serving meat, or not inviting vegetarians. However, alternative options might be to serve vegetarians the same meal but without the meat, or cook fabulous vegetarian food that wouldn't disappoint anyone".

Post Hoc reasoning argues that *A Caused B* just because *A* happened *First*

1) If two events have a **causal relation**, it means **one** was **caused** by the **other** one. There are **three** ways that an **argument** might **confuse** causal relations — **post hoc**, **simplifying** causal relations, and **confusing** cause and effect.

2) Post Hoc is when an argument **claims** that event A **caused** event B, but actually event A only **happened before** event B.

3) **Even** if event A **did** cause event B, this reasoning is always flawed because no other **evidence** is given to persuade us that one **caused** the other. **More information** is needed before we can accept the conclusion. E.g.

> It's obvious that doing tax rebates and audits didn't cause the weight loss — the weight loss just happened to occur after he started doing them.

> After he started working as an accountant, he lost weight. Therefore calculating tax rebates and looking at company audits is a good way to lose weight.

> After he stopped having burger and chips for breakfast every day, he lost weight. Therefore, eating a burger and chips for breakfast was making him fat.

> This is probably true — but it uses exactly the same reasoning as the first argument, so it still commits the Post Hoc flaw. More reasons are needed to support the claim.

4) This flaw is also known as a **false cause**.

There are *Two Different Ways* of *Simplifying Causal Relations*

1) If an argument claims that one thing was **entirely responsible** for making something happen, when actually **several** factors **combined** to cause the **result**, it's called "**simplifying causal relations**". E.g.

> The prime minister's financial policies were over-ambitious, and that's what caused the economy to collapse. If we'd elected someone else then the economy would still be flourishing.

← Many factors affect the economy, including the economies of other countries and decisions made by banks.

2) It's also called **simplifying causal relations** if the argument claims that event A **caused** event B, when actually they're **both caused** by event C. E.g. "Annual figures show that as sales of ice cream go up, the number of drowning incidents also increases. This shows that ice cream affects your ability to swim."

3) Both these things actually **increase** in the **summer**, because the **hot weather** encourages more people to go swimming (which leads to an increase in drowning incidents), and also makes people more likely to buy ice cream. So it's the **weather** that's the **cause** of the **increases** in both ice cream sales and drowning incidents.

Confusing Cause and *Effect* means getting them the *Wrong Way Round*

For example:
> Stuart has the flu a lot more than I do — I think it's because he visits the doctor's surgery more often than me. The waiting room must be full of germs and that's why he catches more viruses.

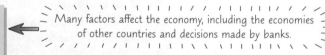
It's more likely that Stuart's frequent visits to the doctor are caused by him having the flu, not that the flu is caused by the visits.

Flaws

You'll have to Identify and Explain the Different Flaws

1) In the **exam**, there are **three kinds** of **questions** about flaws that come up a lot.

2) In **multiple choice** questions, you'll probably have to **choose** the **correct name** for the flawed reasoning — which tests your ability to **recognise** and **name** flaws in an argument. E.g.

> Q1 "Homeopathy is a miracle cure. My dog was often aggressive and would bite for no reason. But after I started feeding her homeopathic pills, she calmed down and is now friendly and docile."
>
> The argument above contains a flaw in its reasoning.
> Which term best describes this flaw?
>
> a) Slippery Slope   c) Post Hoc
> b) Conflation   d) Circular Argument

Some flaws are easier to identify than others...

3) In Section B, you might be asked to **recognise** the flaw in the passage and **also** give an **explanation** of why it's flawed. This needs a longer answer. For example:

> Q2 The reasoning in the passage above is flawed. Name the flaw and explain why it causes the reasoning to fail, with specific reference to the argument's reasoning.

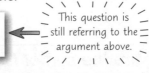

This question is still referring to the argument above.

4) It's important to **name** the flaw, explain **why** the reasoning is flawed and **relate** your explanation to the passage. E.g.

- This doesn't **clearly state** the name of the flaw, or explain the flaw in the reasoning.

  → There could be another cause for the reduction of the dog's aggressive behaviour.

- This **explains** the flaw but doesn't **refer** specifically to the argument.

  → This is a post hoc flaw — the two events happened one after the other, but that doesn't support the reasoning that one was caused by the other.

- This is **good** — it correctly **names** the flaw, makes reference to the argument, and **explains** why the flaw causes the reasoning to fail.

  → This is a post hoc flaw — just because the use of homeopathic pills happened before the reduction in aggressive behaviour, doesn't support the claim that the homeopathic pills caused the dog to calm down.

5) You might also be asked to give an **evaluation** of the **reasoning** in an argument — considering **flaws**, **examples**, **evidence** and **other** argument **elements**. For a **worked answer** on a question like this, see p.73.

Practice Questions

Q1   Name the flaw in the following argument:

"If you want to be successful, you either have to be very talented or prepared to be completely ruthless to stamp out any competition. I'm not talented, so the only way I'm going to succeed is by being ruthless and cruel."

Exam Question

Q1   Name the flaw in the reasoning below, and explain why the reasoning doesn't work, referring specifically to the text.

"After someone starts receiving Job Seeker's Allowance, they frequently feel sad and start to believe there's no hope of finding another job. So giving people benefits makes them depressed and unmotivated."

[3 marks]

You can't stand on a perfect argument — it's flawless...

When I first learnt about Post Hoc and causal relations, I was absolutely baffled. Why casual? Are the events just going on the occasional date but not meeting each other's parents? It took me three months to see it was written CAUS-al — as in CAUSE. Causal, not casual. Anyway, you're probably not as silly as me, but I thought I'd make that clear, just in case...

Appeals to Emotion & Authority

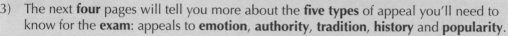

Understanding appeals is trickier than eating jelly with chopsticks — sometimes they're flaws and sometimes they're not. I wish they'd just make their minds up. Thankfully the next four pages are here to help you avoid any sticky disappointing messes...

Appeals **Persuade** people that a **Conclusion** is true using **Emotional Persuasion**

1) Some arguments use **appeals** to try and **convince** people that their conclusion is true by using **emotional persuasion** instead of **reasons**.

> *Weak appeals are sometimes called **irrelevant** or **inappropriate** appeals.*

2) Using an **appeal** means referring to things like **popularity** or **tradition** to persuade us that a conclusion is true. Sometimes this can **seem** very **convincing**, but actually it might **not support** the **conclusion** at all.

3) The next **four** pages will tell you more about the **five types** of appeal you'll need to know for the **exam**: appeals to **emotion**, **authority**, **tradition**, **history** and **popularity**.

4) At AS-level you'll probably **only** see **weak** appeals, which don't support the conclusion. You'll need to be able to spot them and know how to explain **why** they're weak. There's also **more** about this on the next **four** pages.

5) Weak appeals are a type of **flaw** because they **don't** support the conclusion.

These are the sort of **Exam Questions** you'll get about **Appeals**

Q1 'The council is discussing plans to build a bypass around the village. This would have a negative effect on the local economy. When a bypass was built around West Wisbury three years ago, the amount of money spent in local shops halved.' What is the name of the appeal contained in this argument?
(a) Appeal to emotion
(b) Appeal to history
(c) Appeal to tradition
(d) Appeal to authority

Q2 Read the source document in the resource booklet. Name a flaw in the third paragraph, and explain why it is a flaw. You should refer to the argument's reasoning in your answer.

Appeals to **Emotion** use people's **Feelings** to **Persuade** them

1) Appeals to **emotion** try to get us to believe a particular **outcome** will happen **just** because we have an **emotional response** to the argument, not because we're **convinced** by its **reasons**.

2) Appeals to emotion can often be **spotted** by looking out for **emotive language** — **words** and **phrases** that try to bring out an **emotional response** in people, e.g. using the word '**havoc**' instead of the word '**problems**', the word '**riot**' instead of '**disturbance**', or '**slaughtered**' instead of '**killed**'.

Mark used appeals to emotion from a very young age.

Appeals to emotion **Support** the conclusion if the **Outcome** is **Likely**

1) If the **outcome** of the appeal is **likely**, the appeal is **appropriate** — it supports the **conclusion**.

> New 'Pleasant-Smelling Moisturiser' will prevent irritating dry skin and its lovely smell will make you feel pampered. You should buy some today.

> *It doesn't go **against common sense** to believe that a **moisturiser** will prevent dry skin and smell nice. This appeal to **emotion** is **appropriate** and supports the **conclusion** that we 'should buy some today'.*

2) However, if the **outcome** is **unlikely**, the appeal is **inappropriate** — it **doesn't** support the conclusion.

> New 'Time-Reverse' anti-wrinkle cream will reverse the aging process and make you look as beautiful as this model. You should go out and buy some of this fabulous cream today.

> *You'd have to **abandon common sense** to believe that this cream can really '**reverse the aging process**' so this appeal is **inappropriate**, and doesn't support the **conclusion** that you should 'buy some' today.*

Appeals to Emotion & Authority

Appeals to Authority refer to Experts or people in Charge

1) Appeals to **authority** refer to the **opinions** or **actions** of people in **authority**, e.g. doctors, police officers, politicians.

2) You can **sometimes** spot appeals to **authority** because they contain **quotes** from the **person** in authority.

3) Here's an **example** of an **appeal** to authority:

> The public can now return to the centre of town. According to Detective Constable Richards from the local police's gun control unit, 'The gunmen have all been caught and the area is now safe for the public.'

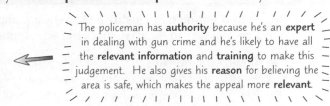

The policeman has **authority** because he's an **expert** in dealing with gun crime and he's likely to have all the **relevant information** and **training** to make this judgement. He also gives his **reason** for believing the area is safe, which makes the appeal more **relevant**.

4) This appeal to **authority** is **relevant** and **appropriate** — the policeman's evidence is a **good reason** to support the **conclusion** that 'The public can now return to the centre of town.'

Appeals to authority don't Strengthen arguments if they don't give Reasons

1) Sometimes appeals to **authority** are **irrelevant** to the argument because we're given no **reason** apart from someone's **authority** to accept what they're saying.

> The Mayor said that the protest should be allowed, therefore we're going to let it go ahead.

The fact that the **Mayor** has said the protest should be allowed is not a good **reason** to let it go ahead. This is a **weak appeal** because we don't know what his **reasons** are and even experts are **wrong** sometimes.

2) But if we add the Mayor's **reasons**, this **strengthens** the argument — the reasons **support** the conclusion and they come from an **expert**.

> The Mayor said that the protest should be allowed because it will let people show their anger in a constructive way. He added that there will be a large police presence to make sure that there's no violence. Therefore we're going to let it go ahead.

George decided to try a new way of getting people to respect his authority.

Practice Questions

Q1 What is an appeal to authority?

Q2 'The wind farm obviously shouldn't be built here. We don't want our beautiful views of the rolling hills and calm fields spoilt by huge ugly turbines. They're a blight on the landscape and we cannot allow the council to destroy our surroundings any longer.'
What is the name of the flaw in the passage above?
(a) Slippery slope (b) Tu quoque (c) Irrelevant appeal to emotion (d) Irrelevant appeal to authority.

Q3 Why does the flaw in question 2 not support the conclusion?

Exam Question

Q1 It's not safe for pregnant women to use this drug. GPs and hospitals should no longer prescribe it to women of childbearing age. Mr. Gregson, a consultant at Summerview Hospital, said, "The drug should not be used until further studies have been carried out on its effects."

Name the flaw in this argument and explain why it is flawed. [3 marks]

My flawed breakfast — I was a-peelin' my banana when I got a bit emotional...

Sorry about that, I just can't help myself sometimes... Anyway, the important thing to take from these two pages is that it's not enough to know whether an appeal is irrelevant or inappropriate — you've got to be able to say WHY. I know it's annoying but there it is — examiners aren't here to make friends, they're here to test your critical thinking skills so make sure you keep them happy.

Appeals to Tradition, History & Popularity

These two pages cover three more appeals: appeals to tradition, history and popularity. A little warning — it's not always easy to tell the difference between these appeals, especially appeals to tradition and history. Make sure you can tell them apart.

Appeals to *Tradition* refer to the *Way* things have *Always Been*

1) Appeals to **tradition** try to **justify** a claim by arguing that **just** because something's been done a certain way in the **past**, that's the way it should be done in the **future**. E.g.

> We should continue to serve the elderly residents of the care home their meals at the same time of day. That's when they've always eaten in the past.

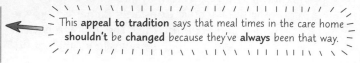
This **appeal to tradition** says that meal times in the care home **shouldn't be changed** because they've **always** been that way.

Appeals to *Tradition* often aren't *Supported* by *Reasons*

1) Appeals to **tradition** on their **own** don't **support** arguments very well. **Just** because something's been done a certain way in the **past** doesn't mean it should **continue** to be done that way in the **future**. The **situation** might have **changed** or it might **always** have been the **wrong** way to do it.

2) In the example above, the **conclusion** that 'we should continue to serve the elderly residents of the care home their meals at the same time of day' **isn't** supported by the **reason** that it's 'when they've always eaten in the past' so the **appeal** is **irrelevant** and doesn't **support** the **conclusion**.

3) These appeals can be **relevant** if they're followed by an extra **reason** saying **why** the tradition is **important**:

> We should continue to serve the elderly residents of the care home their meals at the same time of day. That's when they've always eaten in the past and a strict routine makes them feel safe and keeps them healthy.

The example now gives a **reason why** the tradition should be **kept** — it's better for the health and happiness of the residents. This is a **relevant** appeal to tradition.

Appeals to *History* use what's *Already* happened to *Predict* what *Will* happen

1) Appeals to history **assume** that because something's **usually** happened a certain way in the **past**, it'll also **happen** that way in the **future**. E.g.

> It's never taken me more than an hour to get home so I'll definitely be there before 7:30.

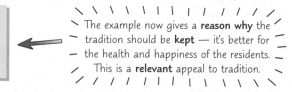
Past events ('it's never taken me more than an hour to get home') are being used to **predict** what'll happen in the **future** ('I'll definitely be there before 7:30').

2) You can **spot** appeals to history because they say something has **usually** happened a certain way in the past, or has **never** happened differently: 'It **never** takes me more than an hour to get home,' 'She **normally** wins races so she'll win this race.'

The *Past* isn't always a *Reliable* guide to the *Future*

1) Appeals to history often **seem** really **convincing** — in **everyday** life we **often** assume that things that were true in the **past** will still be true in the **future**, e.g. the sun will rise **tomorrow** because it always has in the **past**.

2) But appeals to history are often **too weak** to really support an argument. The **reason**, 'It's never taken me more than an hour to get home,' only gives **weak support** to the **conclusion** 'I'll definitely be there before 7:30'. There are **lots** of things that might happen to **stop** me getting home before 7:30, e.g. a traffic **accident**, a **storm**, my car **breaking down**.

3) But appeals to history can give **strong** support to a conclusion that says something will **probably** happen.

> It's never taken me more than an hour to get home so I'll **probably** be there before 7:30.

4) Appeals to history are also **stronger** if they're based on **lots** of evidence from the **past**. Here's an example that is backed up by lots of **evidence**, and uses '**probably**' in its conclusion — this appeal to history is **relevant**.

> Girls have performed better than boys in GCSE exams every year for more than two decades. Therefore they will probably perform better this year as well.

Appeals to Tradition, History & Popularity

Appeals to **Popularity** say a conclusion is **True** because **Lots** of people **Believe** it

1) These appeals **refer** to a conclusion's **popularity** to convince people that it **must** be true.

2) Here's an **example** of an appeal to **popularity**:

> The Shed-Kleen is the must-have shed cleaning product of the year. It's already used by four million shed-owners in the UK. Every shed-owner should buy themselves a Shed-Kleen.

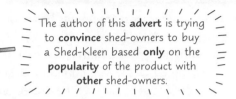

The author of this **advert** is trying to **convince** shed-owners to buy a Shed-Kleen based **only** on the **popularity** of the product with **other** shed-owners.

3) Appeals to **popularity** are easy to spot because they **always** refer to a **large** number of **people** e.g. 'four million shed-owners' or 'four out of five people' or '78%'.

Lots of people can **Believe** something that is **Wrong**

1) Saying that **many people** believe something **doesn't** make it true — lots of people can **still** be **wrong**. E.g. until the 16th century, **most people** believed the **earth** was the **centre** of the **universe**.

2) The **example** above doesn't give any **details** about the Shed-Kleen or any **reasons** why it's a good product. The appeal to **popularity** is **irrelevant** to the conclusion that shed-owners **should** buy one.

3) But appeals to popularity **can** be **useful** if something's popularity is **relevant** to the conclusion. E.g.

> The Shed-Kleen is the must-have shed cleaning product of the year. It's already used by four million shed-owners in the UK. It is a popular product so we would sell more copies of *Shedlovers' Magazine* if we wrote about it.

The **popularity** of the Shed-Kleen is **important** to the editors of a **magazine** for shed lovers as they want to write about things that **interest** their readers. Here, the **appeal** to popularity **supports** the conclusion.

Bernard's 'interesting' hobby meant he had no popularity to appeal to.

Practice Questions

Q1 What's the difference between an appeal to history and an appeal to tradition?

Q2 'Of course we need the Royal Family. Great Britain has had a monarch for nearly a thousand years and we're one of the only countries in the world that has been true to its roots and not become a republic.' What's the name of the appeal used in the passage above?
(a) Appeal to history (b) Appeal to tradition (c) Appeal to emotion (d) Appeal to popularity.

Q3 Why does the appeal in question 2 not support the conclusion?

Q4 Why do appeals to popularity often not support an argument's conclusion?

Exam Question

Q1 "A recent poll was carried out to discover whether people in the UK wished to remain part of the European Union. 70% of people polled replied that they thought the UK should stay in the EU, and 20% did not vote. Only 10% said that they wanted the UK to leave the EU. Therefore, the Government should make sure that we remain in the EU."

Name the flaw in this argument and explain why it is flawed.

[3 marks]

I bet you thought there'd be a joke here — you can't rely on appeals to history...

Congratulations — you've finally reached the end of the longest section in the book. It was a bit of a mammoth of a section, but full of really useful bits and bobs. The most important thing to remember is that flaws are always illogical — they always weaken an argument. Appeals can be flaws if they're irrelevant, but stronger appeals can also support an argument's conclusion... Tricky.

What You'll Have To Do

Now you know the different elements of an argument, it's time to start writing your own. This is a pretty tricky part of the exam — this section will help by taking you step-by-step through an argument to show how it's done. So "here's one I wrote earlier..."

You'll have to **Write** your **Own Argument**

1) In Unit 2 you'll have to write your **own arguments** based on source material.

2) You'll be given a **conclusion** or **claim** and you'll have to either **support** or **challenge** it. The conclusion or claim might be taken **straight** from the **source** material or it might just be on the same **topic**.

3) The **question** will say something like "You should include at least **three reasons**, an **intermediate conclusion** and a **main conclusion**." You've **got** to include **these** elements in your argument or you **can't** get full marks.

4) You can also add **other** argument elements. Just **remember** — **don't** use an element unless it **improves** your argument. Don't add extra elements just for the **sake** of it.

5) Try to add **argument indicators** like 'therefore' and 'in addition' — this'll make your argument really **clear**.

6) The next five pages will **show** you how to **add** argument elements one at a time.

The **Source Material** will look something like this

Read this **source** document then have a look at the question below.

> Illegal downloads are crippling the UK's music industry and creating a generation of teenagers who are indifferent to criminal acts. The government should make it a priority to eradicate this kind of crime and punish those involved.   1
>
> Record companies and artists lose billions of pounds in revenue every year because people are sharing their songs online instead of paying for them. File sharing is not illegal, but sharing copyright files, like music tracks, is. A lot of money and hard work goes into producing these songs, and it's not fair that people are downloading them for free. In the UK, six million people share files illegally, and this goes largely unpunished.   2
>
> By allowing this kind of piracy to continue, the government is sending a clear message to a generation of teenagers that this crime is not really a crime. No one gets punished, so it must be acceptable to steal in this way. This is a dangerous impression to give – Internet piracy can start these young people on a path towards more serious crimes, like shoplifting and burglary. We need to take action to prevent this.   3
>
> The best way of dealing with this problem is to shut down illegal file-sharing websites. A survey last month showed that since file-sharing technology became available, the number of websites using this technology has grown every year. Record companies have started to sue the owners of these websites, and some have already been forced to shut down. Some website owners have been sent to prison, as well as being fined hundreds of millions of pounds. These website owners argue that they aren't doing anything wrong – that they're just hosting the files and it's the public who are breaking the law by sharing them – but this is just an excuse. The administrators of these sites know that copyright files are being shared, and they have been allowing this to go on without trying to stop it.   4
>
> Shutting down illegal file-sharing websites is the best way of tackling the problem of illegal downloads, so the police need to focus on prosecuting the owners of these sites, and making sure the record companies and artists are paid the compensation that they deserve.   5

Be Careful when you're Challenging a claim

1) If you're writing an argument **supporting** a claim, use that **exact** claim as your **conclusion**.

2) If your argument needs to **challenge** a claim, writing your conclusion is a bit more **tricky**. It must **disagree** with the **claim**. Here are some **examples**:

Income tax should be **increased**.	• Income tax should **not** be **increased**. • Income tax should be **reduced**. • Income tax should stay the **same**.
Cars are **essential** for families.	• Cars are **not essential** for families. • Cars are **luxuries** for families.

Worked Answer

Read the question Carefully

Q1   Write your own argument to **challenge** the following claim from paragraph 5:

"Shutting down illegal file-sharing websites is the best way of tackling the problem of illegal downloads."

Your argument should be well-structured and developed. You should include at least three reasons, an intermediate conclusion and a main conclusion. Your argument may also include other argument elements.

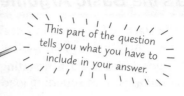
This part of the question tells you what you have to include in your answer.

Use your General Knowledge to think up your Argument

1)   You'll need to come up with **your own** reasons to **challenge** the conclusion.
2)   You **can** use the source for **inspiration**, but it's better if you can think up your **own** reasons.
3)   The examiner doesn't expect you to know **everything** about the topic. You just need to think of some **sensible** and **realistic** reasons to challenge the **conclusion** you've been given.

Plan your Argument before you start

1)   Take a couple of **minutes** to write a **quick** plan.
2)   You could use **common notation** to indicate the different **elements** of the argument (see p.4).
3)   Make sure you've **included everything** the examiner's asked for. **Then** if you want to you can **add** extra **elements**.
4)   Here's an **example** of a plan for an answer to the question above:

You need to make it clear from the beginning what the argument's about. Starting with a counter-argument or your conclusion is a good way to do this — starting with reasons usually sounds quite confusing.

CA	Best way to tackle is shutting down websites
R	Because smaller number of websites than users
C	Shutting down websites is not best way
R	Expensive and slow to take website owners to court
R	Number of websites growing all the time
Ev	Survey — number of websites grows every year
R	Doesn't put off users
Hypothetical Reasoning	If website shuts down, then users find another
R	Punishing users deters others and reduces demand
IC	Punishing users is more effective
General Principle	Everyone who breaks the law should be punished
R	Cheap and easy ways to punish users
Ex	Temporarily disconnected from Internet
C	Shutting down websites is not best way

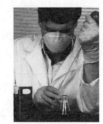
Adding too many extra elements was how One-Eyebrow John got his nickname.

5)   This plan includes **all the elements** you've studied but don't worry — you **don't** have to include them **all** in your argument.
6)   You can change the **order** of the different elements to make your argument more **interesting** — just make sure the argument's still **clear**.

I love sources — ketchup's my favourite...

Coming up with your own arguments may sound terrifying, but don't panic. No one's expecting you to know everything about any topic that might come up in the exam. You just need to use your general knowledge to think of some sensible reasons that relate to the source you've been given. Spend a couple of minutes thinking up ideas and then writing out a quick plan before you start.

Worked Answer

So if you've got your fairy liquid bottle and milk carton handy you can get started on making your very own Tracy Island... er, sorry, I mean argument... Once you've got your plan and your different argument elements, you're ready to start writing.

Here's the **Basic Argument** with three **Reasons** and a **Conclusion**

1) We're **starting** from the most **basic** type of argument — several **reasons** and a **conclusion** — then we'll add **other** elements one at a time.

2) It's a good idea to **start** by **stating** your conclusion. This will keep your argument **focused** as well as **sounding** loads better than launching straight into your **reasons**.

3) Having two **identical** versions of the **conclusion** might sound a bit **odd**, but they'll be much **further apart** when the **rest** of the argument has been **added**.

C — Shutting down illegal file-sharing websites is not the best way of tackling the problem of illegal downloads. Taking the owners of illegal download websites to court is a long and expensive process. In addition, the number of file-sharing websites is increasing all the time, which makes closing them all down impossible. There are also cheap and easy ways of punishing website users without long and expensive court cases. In conclusion, shutting down illegal file-sharing websites is not the best way of tackling the problem of illegal downloads. — C

R1, R2, R3

The argument also **Needs** to have an **Intermediate Conclusion**

1) An intermediate conclusion is a **conclusion** made partway through an argument which **supports** the **main** conclusion — it acts as a **reason** supporting it.

2) It's **supported** by **reasons** just like the main conclusion.

3) Here's an **IC** we can **add** to our argument with two **reasons** to support it:

See p.34 for more about intermediate conclusions.

R	Shutting down these websites doesn't put off individual users.
R	Punishing individual users would deter others and reduce the demand for illegal file-sharing websites.
IC	Punishing website users is a more effective way of solving the problem of illegal downloads.

4) When you're planning, you should **check** that your intermediate conclusion definitely **supports** the main conclusion.

5) Ask yourself whether it gives a **reason** to support the **conclusion**:

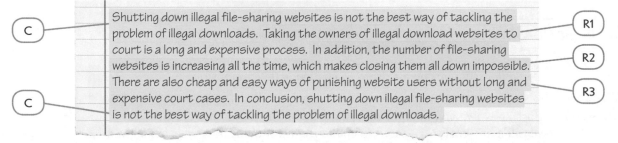

Punishing website users is a more effective way of solving the problem of illegal downloads.

...is a reason to support the conclusion that...

Shutting down illegal file-sharing websites is not the best way of tackling the problem of illegal downloads.

This is what the **Argument Looks** like in **Full**

You can add indicators like, 'Also...' and, 'Therefore...' to make the IC clearer.

Reasons — Shutting down illegal file-sharing websites is not the best way of tackling the problem of illegal downloads. Taking the owners of illegal download websites to court is a long and expensive process. In addition, the number of file-sharing websites is increasing all the time, which makes closing them all down impossible. Also, shutting down these websites doesn't put off individual users. Punishing individual users would deter others and reduce the demand for illegal file-sharing websites. Therefore, punishing website users is a more effective way of solving the problem of illegal downloads. There are also cheap and easy ways of punishing website users without long and expensive court cases. In conclusion, shutting down illegal file-sharing websites is not the best way of tackling the problem of illegal downloads. — IC

Worked Answer

Evidence and Examples help to Support your Reasons

1) **Evidence** and **examples** can be used to **support** an argument.

2) Evidence is **information** that backs up the **reasons** in an argument.

3) Examples are real situations that **illustrate** a reason and make it **clearer**.

4) You only need to use your **general knowledge** to come up with evidence and examples — no one's expecting you to be an **expert**.

5) Just remember — they've got to be **relevant** and **realistic**.

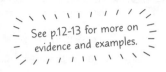
See p.12-13 for more on evidence and examples.

Here's an Example that Supports R1

We've added **information** about another long and expensive **court case** about file sharing as an **example**.

> Shutting down illegal file-sharing websites is not the best way of tackling the problem of illegal downloads. Taking the owners of illegal download websites to court is a long and expensive process. In addition, the number of file-sharing websites is increasing all the time, which makes closing them all down impossible. Also, shutting down these websites doesn't put off individual users. Punishing individual users would deter others and reduce the demand for illegal file-sharing websites. Therefore, punishing website users is a more effective way of solving the problem of illegal downloads. There are also cheap and easy ways of punishing website users without long and expensive court cases. For example they could be temporarily disconnected from the internet. In conclusion, shutting down illegal file-sharing websites is not the best way of tackling the problem of illegal downloads.

(Ex)

Here's some Evidence to Support R2

Here we've added a **statistic** which **backs up** the claim that the number of websites is constantly **increasing**.

(Ev)

> Shutting down illegal file-sharing websites is not the best way of tackling the problem of illegal downloads. Taking the owners of illegal download websites to court is a long and expensive process. In addition, the number of file-sharing websites is increasing all the time, which makes closing them all down impossible. A recent survey has shown that the number of these websites has increased every year since file-sharing technology was developed. Also, shutting down these websites doesn't put off individual users. Punishing individual users would deter others and reduce the demand for illegal file-sharing websites. Therefore, punishing website users is a more effective way of solving the problem of illegal downloads. There are also cheap and easy ways of punishing website users without long and expensive court cases. For example they could be temporarily disconnected from the internet. In conclusion, shutting down illegal file-sharing websites is not the best way of tackling the problem of illegal downloads.

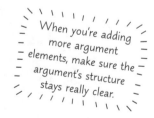
When you're adding more argument elements, make sure the argument's structure stays really clear.

I'm not an intermediate conclusion yet — I'm still just a beginner...

I know all this arguing stuff is pretty thrilling, but don't get carried away and start writing a whole load of waffle just to try and fill the page. Plan your argument carefully and stick to your plan. Your argument doesn't have to be really complicated or very long, it just needs to be clear and focused. Wow, I'm starting to sound like my Mum... It's still good advice though...

Worked Answer

This argument's shaping up pretty well, though I say so myself... Still, there are a few more things you can add to an argument to make it the best darn argument the world has ever seen. These are the last ones though, I promise.

It's easy to add **Counter-Assertions** or **Counter-Arguments**

1) Counter-assertions and counter-arguments **oppose** the main **conclusion**.
2) Counter-assertions are statements **without** reasons to **support** them.
3) Counter arguments are **similar** to counter-assertions, but they're **supported** by a **reason**.
4) **Dismissing** counter-arguments or counter-assertions by giving a **reason** which goes against them can **strengthen** your argument.

See p.8 for more on counter-assertions and counter-arguments.

Here's the **Argument** with a **Counter-Assertion** added

CA

Many people argue that the best way of reducing illegal music downloads is to shut down the websites that allow them. However, shutting down illegal file-sharing websites is not the best way of tackling the problem of illegal downloads. Taking the owners of illegal download websites to court is a long and expensive process. In addition, the number of file-sharing websites is increasing all the time, which makes closing them all down impossible. A recent survey has shown that the number of these websites has increased every year since file-sharing technology was developed. Also, shutting down these websites doesn't put off individual users. Punishing individual users would deter others and reduce the demand for illegal file-sharing websites. Therefore, punishing website users is a more effective way of solving the problem of illegal downloads. There are also cheap and easy ways of punishing website users without long and expensive court cases. For example they could be temporarily disconnected from the internet. In conclusion, shutting down illegal file-sharing websites is not the best way of tackling the problem of illegal downloads.

'However' is an indicator word that shows the counter-assertion is being dismissed.

Here we've added a **Reason** so it becomes a **Counter-Argument**

CA

Many people argue that the best way of reducing illegal music downloads is to shut down the websites that allow them. This is because the number of websites is far smaller than the number of people using them. However, shutting down illegal file-sharing websites is not the best way of tackling the problem of illegal downloads. Taking the owners of illegal download websites to court is a long and expensive process. In addition, the number of file-sharing websites is increasing all the time, which makes closing them all down impossible. A recent survey has shown that the number of these websites has increased every year since file-sharing technology was developed. Also, shutting down these websites doesn't put off individual users. Punishing individual users would deter others and reduce the demand for illegal file-sharing websites. Therefore, punishing website users is a more effective way of solving the problem of illegal downloads. There are also cheap and easy ways of punishing website users without long and expensive court cases. For example they could be temporarily disconnected from the internet. In conclusion, shutting down illegal file-sharing websites is not the best way of tackling the problem of illegal downloads.

The counter-argument was getting heated — Marjorie was certain she'd counted two tiddlywinks.

Worked Answer

Hypothetical Reasoning *can be used as a* Reason

1) Hypothetical reasoning has the structure **'if...... then.....'**
2) It's a **prediction** about what'll happen in the future that **depends** on something else.
3) Here's how it can be used in this **argument**:

See p.9 for more on hypothetical reasoning.

> Many people argue that the best way of reducing illegal music downloads is to shut down the websites that allow them. This is because the number of websites is far smaller than the number of people using them. However, shutting down illegal file-sharing websites is not the best way of tackling the problem of illegal downloads. Taking the owners of illegal download websites to court is a long and expensive process. In addition, the number of file-sharing websites is increasing all the time, which makes closing them all down impossible. A recent survey has shown that the number of these websites has increased every year since file-sharing technology was developed. Also, shutting down these websites doesn't put off individual users. **If one website is shut down then its users can just start visiting a different one.** Punishing individual users would deter others and reduce the demand for illegal file-sharing websites. Therefore, punishing website users is a more effective way of solving the problem of illegal downloads. There are also cheap and easy ways of punishing website users without long and expensive court cases. For example they could be temporarily disconnected from the internet. In conclusion, shutting down illegal file-sharing websites is not the best way of tackling the problem of illegal downloads.

Hypothetical Reasoning

General Principles *can also be used as* Reasons

1) General principles are **rules** to **guide** how we act
   — they can be **moral**, **social**, **legal** or **practical**.
2) They **apply** to **many** different situations.
3) You might need to **add** a few words to **introduce** your general principle:

Look back at p.40 on general principles.

> Many people argue that the best way of reducing illegal music downloads is to shut down the websites that allow them. This is because the number of websites is far smaller than the number of people using them. However, shutting down illegal file-sharing websites is not the best way of tackling the problem of illegal downloads. Taking the owners of illegal download websites to court is a long and expensive process. In addition, the number of file-sharing websites is increasing all the time, which makes closing them all down impossible. A recent survey has shown that the number of these websites has increased every year since file-sharing technology was developed. Also, shutting down these websites doesn't put off individual users. If one website is shut down then its users can just start visiting a different one. Punishing individual users would deter others and reduce the demand for illegal file-sharing websites. Therefore, punishing website users is a more effective way of solving the problem of illegal downloads, **especially as using these websites is illegal and everyone who breaks the law should be punished.** There are also cheap and easy ways of punishing website users without long and expensive court cases. For example they could be temporarily disconnected from the internet. In conclusion, shutting down illegal file-sharing websites is not the best way of tackling the problem of illegal downloads.

General Principle

General Principle is on his way to talk to the troops now, sir...

So that's it, argument — done. Remember, these pages are just here to show you how to add the different elements. Don't go adding them all into an argument at once just for the sake of it. Always use all the elements the examiner's asked for in the question but only add others if they definitely improve your argument. You won't get any marks for irrelevant elements.

Do Well in Unit One

This last section contains advice about how to do fantastically in the exam, as well as lots of sample answers. In the resource booklet for Unit 1 you'll find some background information, one main source and two or three other sources like the ones on these two pages.

This page contains **Background Information** and the **Main Resource**

Background information

The number of students taking a GCSE exam in a modern language has been falling since 2001. In 2010, to try to stop the decline in the study of languages, as well as other 'serious' academic subjects, the government introduced a new award, known as the English Baccalaureate, or EBacc for short. To be awarded the EBacc, students have to achieve A*- C grades in five core subjects, including an ancient or modern language. Currently, the majority of students study French, Spanish or German as their language, but in the last year, the number of entries for GCSE Mandarin Chinese has risen by more than 5%.

Document 1

All students should be offered Chinese lessons

The UK government has announced new plans to address the decline in the number of pupils studying core subjects at GCSE level. Since 2001, the number of pupils attaining five A*- C grades in GCSE exams including maths, science, English and a foreign language has fallen every year, and the biggest decline is in foreign languages. In an attempt to boost the number of pupils taking core subjects, especially languages, the government's new English Baccalaureate award will recognise pupils who achieve A*- C grades in maths, English, a science, a humanity, and a language. The number of pupils attaining the 'EBacc' will appear on school league tables, giving teachers an incentive to encourage pupils to study these subjects. Although students traditionally study a European language at GCSE, the government has singled out Mandarin Chinese as a particularly desirable language. The Education Secretary recently announced new plans to increase the number of Mandarin Chinese teachers by more than a thousand by 2016, to cope with increasing demand for these lessons in schools.   1

This government focus on languages, and on Mandarin Chinese in particular, should be supported, but it should be taken even further. The advantages of learning Mandarin are so great that all children should be given the opportunity to do so. Many experts have called for improvements in the standard of English grammar, and learning another language can increase a child's awareness of how they use their own. Of course, children can improve their grasp of English by learning any language, including those that are traditionally taught in this country such as French and German, but we should aim to inspire children by giving them the chance to learn a completely new language, one that they are unlikely to have had any experience of before.   2

Critics of this plan argue that children should continue to learn European languages because children from poorer backgrounds will inevitably fall behind in Mandarin Chinese lessons. They say that schools teaching French can organise relatively inexpensive trips to France so pupils can immerse themselves in the language, but trips to China are far too expensive for all but the richest families. However, modern technology means that pupils can access Mandarin Chinese resources over the internet, and could even interact with native Chinese children online. It is now much easier to learn about other countries without the crippling expense of travelling to the other side of the world.   3

China is among the world's largest economies, as well as one of its fastest growing. The UK can no longer ignore the fact that China is, and will remain, a major global economic power. British companies increasingly need to trade with China so, for the sake of our economy, we must respond to China's growth by teaching our children to conduct business in Mandarin.   4

The government's proposals to encourage language teaching are commendable, but they do not go far enough. Rather than giving only some children the opportunity to learn Mandarin Chinese, surely they all deserve this chance. The advantages of learning Mandarin at school are so great that the government should aim to introduce Mandarin Chinese lessons to all secondary schools in the UK.   5

Document 2

Reactions to the article

Professor Jonathan Leadbeater, Head of European Languages at the University of Spellton, disagrees with the proposals to make Mandarin Chinese available to all school-age children. He says: 'While it is commendable that the government is acting to increase the uptake of languages in schools, universities are simply not equipped to deal with a large influx of students wishing to study Mandarin Chinese. Other, well established language departments will be forced to close if their funding is used to set up Chinese departments instead. It would be better for the government to encourage more children to learn European languages.'   6

Sally Franks, a headteacher from Somerset, reacted positively to the government's proposals: 'GCSE students will find it really inspiring to have the opportunity to learn Mandarin Chinese. Two years ago our school was one of ten schools in the South West that replaced GCSE French with GCSE Portuguese because pupils found French boring. Now, 30% more pupils in all of these schools achieve an A*- C grade in Portuguese than they did in French. I think learning Chinese would have a similar effect on pupils across the country.'   7

Mrs. Whittal, the mother of a girl already studying Mandarin Chinese at GCSE, argues, 'I studied French at university so I could have helped Joanna with her homework if she was doing French, but I haven't got the foggiest idea about Chinese. Nights when she has Chinese homework are very stressful because she finds it really hard and when she doesn't understand something I can't help her with it. It's better to stick with what people know.'   8

Document 3

Learning Chinese makes people more employable

Recent proposals to increase provision for Mandarin Chinese teaching in British schools should be supported. Chinese speakers are almost as much in demand as French speakers in today's businesses, and yet far more students study French. Companies are reporting a real shortage of Chinese speakers so students leaving school with the ability to converse in Mandarin are instantly more employable.   9

Large corporations based in the UK are increasingly doing business with China and those represented by the UK Federation of Graduate Employers are no exception. When asked whether having a grade A in Mandarin Chinese GCSE would significantly improve a graduate's chances of securing a job with them, 90% replied that it would.   10

With increasing numbers of graduates flooding the international job market, it is vital that graduates have something on their CV to distinguish them from other candidates. Mandarin Chinese is the ideal qualification to make someone stand out from the crowd.   11

UK Federation of Graduate Recruiters (UFGR)
We act as an intermediary body between graduates and the corporations looking to employ them. Employers want a better quality of graduate with the correct skillset for their organisation, and graduates want to know which job is right for them and how to get it. We aim to facilitate both of these objectives.

"May the Source be with you..."

All the questions in the paper are based on the documents in your resource booklet so you have to read them pretty carefully. If you like, you can underline important bits or use common notation to label the argument elements. Spend about 10 minutes reading the sources before you start — it'll make the questions easier to answer. There are some sample answers on the next few pages...

Do Well in Unit One — Section A

The next three pages give you some advice about how to answer some of the questions that are likely to come up in the Unit 1 exam, and we've included some sample answers too. The sample answers are based on the sources on p.66-67.

Some **Questions** will ask you to 'State....'

1) If the question asks you to 'state', the examiner wants you to **quote** directly from the **document**.

2) You'll **lose** marks for **paraphrasing** (putting the answer in your **own** words), or for **missing** out parts of the answer.

---

1. (a)   Look at Document 1. State the main conclusion of the argument in this document. In your answer you should use the exact words found in the document.   [3 marks]

> The UK government needs to give all children the chance to learn Chinese.

Don't **paraphrase** — copy the **exact words** in the document.

> The government should aim to introduce Mandarin Chinese lessons to all secondary schools in the UK.

---

1. (b)   State one reason found in paragraph 4 of Document 1.   [3 marks]

> British companies increasingly need to trade with China so, for the sake of our economy, we must respond to China's growth by teaching our children to conduct business in Mandarin.

Don't **include** any **extra** elements — you'll **lose** marks.

> British companies increasingly need to trade with China.

\\ \ | | / / /
Questions in Section B will often ask you to 'identify' a claim. 'Identify' means the same as 'state'.
/ / | | \ \ \

Some **Questions** will ask you to 'Explain...'

1) **Explaining** something means saying **why** it's the case.

2) You need to include more **detail** than you would for 'state' questions.

3) Here's one type of **explain** question you might be asked:

Freddie always reacted badly when he was asked to explain himself.

\\ \ | | / /
In Unit 2 you might be asked to 'justify' your answer. This just means 'explain'.
/ / | | \ \

2.   Look at the first sentence of paragraph 3 in Document 1: 'Critics of this plan argue that children should continue to learn European languages because children from poorer backgrounds will inevitably fall behind in Mandarin Chinese lessons.'
(a) Name the argument element.   [2 marks]
(b) Explain your answer to 2(a).   [2 marks]

(a)	Counter-argument.
(b)	It is an argument that goes against the main conclusion.

You don't have to write **lots** to get the **marks** — just make sure your explanation is **right**.

Do Well in Unit One — Section A

Some *Questions* will ask you to '*Suggest reasons...*'

1) Sometimes you'll have to **suggest** an **additional** reason to support an argument's conclusion.
2) You'll need to use your **general knowledge** to think up a completely **new** reason —
   you won't get any marks for **repeating** reasons that are **already** used in the document.

> 3. Look at the conclusion of the counter-argument found in paragraph 3 of
>   Document 1: 'Children should continue to learn European languages.'
>   Suggest **one** more **reason** to support the claim that it would be better
>   for children to learn European languages rather than Mandarin Chinese.   [3 marks]

Questions in Unit 2 which ask you to 'Give two reasons...' are asking the same thing.

A large percentage of the UK's trade is with businesses in European countries like France and Germany.

The question asks for **one reason** so if you include an **example** like this, you'll **lose marks**.

A large percentage of the UK's trade is with businesses in European countries.

This answer gives a **reason without** including any **unnecessary** information so it would get **full** marks.

Some *Questions* will ask you to '*Assess...*'

1) You'll probably answer a **longer** question asking you to **assess** how well **reasons** support an argument's **conclusion**.
2) These questions are usually **worth** lots of **marks** so it's worth **thinking** about what to **write** before you start.

> 4. Look at Document 3. Assess how far the reasons given in this document support its main conclusion.
>   You should make two developed points and refer directly to two reasons and the conclusion.   [6 marks]

When used alone, the reason in paragraph 10: 'Large corporations based in the UK are increasingly doing business with China' only weakly supports the conclusion that 'recent proposals to increase provision for Mandarin Chinese teaching in British schools should be supported.' Many children will have no ambitions to work for a large corporation, so this reason does not tell us why children in general should learn Mandarin.

The reason in paragraph 11 that states: 'With increasing numbers of graduates flooding the international job market, it is vital that graduates have something on their CV to distinguish them from other candidates' does offer support to the conclusion that the proposals 'should be supported'. The objective of education is to prepare pupils for a career so any subject which increases their chances of getting a good job should be taught to school pupils.

You need to **refer** to **both** the **reason** and the **conclusion** for **every** point you make — **quote** them if you can.

Remember to talk about the **link** between the **reason** and the **conclusion** — say how **well** each reason **supports** the conclusion and **explain why**.

Do Well in Unit One — Section B

Here's how to judge Relative Plausibility and Credibility

1) You'll probably get a **question** that asks you to **compare** the **plausibility** and **credibility** of two **sides** of a debate.

2) You need to write about **four** things — the **plausibility** of **one** side and plausibility of the **other** side, then the **credibility** of **one** side and the credibility of the **other** side.

3) Jot down a **quick plan** of your ideas to help **structure** your answer.

4) These questions are quite **tricky** so here's a **worked example** for you:

> 5. Refer to all the documents in the resource booklet and make a judgement as to whether introducing compulsory Mandarin Chinese lessons would have a positive effect on the education of children in the UK. Your judgement should be based on:
>
> • the relative plausibility (likelihood) of the two outcomes
>
> • the relative credibility of the two sides

The answer starts by discussing the plausibility of the side arguing that learning Mandarin will have a negative effect.

Remember to use quotes if you can.

The first paragraph concludes by saying which is more plausible.

Introducing compulsory Mandarin Chinese lessons could create difficulties for the education system. Schools would need to purchase new teaching resources such as books and software which would cost them thousands of pounds. This means it is quite plausible that it would have a negative effect on students because it would take money away from other subjects and facilities. However, it is likely that the government will provide extra funding for this scheme as they have 'singled out Mandarin Chinese as a particularly desirable language'. Also, while learning Mandarin Chinese, children would also learn about Chinese culture, which is very different from their own. This would enrich their education and make them more aware of other traditions so it is quite plausible that it would have a positive effect on pupils in the UK. Therefore, it is more plausible that compulsory Mandarin Chinese lessons will have a positive effect on the education of children in the UK.

For more on plausibility, see p.20.

The answer then discusses the plausibility of the side arguing that learning Mandarin will have a positive effect.

Remember to explain the credibility criteria you're using.

The paragraph then assesses the credibility of the side arguing that Mandarin lessons will have a positive effect.

As Head of European Languages at a university, Professor Leadbeater has expertise in higher education, but he also has a vested interest in children learning European languages rather than Chinese, as he doesn't want 'well established language departments,' presumably including his own, to close. This decreases the credibility of his objection to the plans. The 'Federation of Graduate Recruiters' has expertise in the graduate recruitment business, but this is not very relevant as their expertise relates only to children who go on to study at university, not to all children in the UK. This decreases the credibility of their claims that learning Mandarin would have a positive effect. As a headmistress of a school, Sally Franks has relevant expertise and experience of the results of a similar language scheme which 'replaced GCSE French with GCSE Portuguese.' She also has a vested interest in maintaining a good reputation as the headteacher of a school. These criteria increase her credibility. Therefore, the side arguing that the proposals will have a positive effect on children's education in the UK is the most credible.

The second paragraph begins by assessing the credibility of the side arguing that Mandarin lessons will have a negative effect.

*Remember to say whether each credibility criterion **increases** or **decreases** credibility.*

The second paragraph concludes by saying which side is more credible.

Don't forget to finish with a main conclusion containing your final judgement about both plausibility and credibility.

In conclusion, compulsory Chinese lessons will probably have a positive effect on the education of children in the UK as this side of the argument is both the most plausible and the most credible.

My relatives are very credible — especially my Gran...

Some of these answers are pretty long — remember to look at the number of marks and the space you're given to work out how much you need to say. If you can't answer a question, don't waste time staring at it — move on and if you've got time at the end, come back to it and have another go. This might seem obvious but it's easy to forget when you're actually in the exam...

Do Well in Unit Two

The next four pages are all about Unit 2. There's a source document just like the one you'll get in the resource booklet and there are lots of sample answers showing you how to tackle the questions you'll see in sections B and C of Unit 2. Remember to have a go at the multiple choice questions on the CD that comes with this book to give you lots of practice for section A of the exam too...

This **Source Document** is like the one you'll get in **Unit Two**

1) Spend about **five minutes** reading the source document on this page — that's **about** how long you'll have in the **exam**.

2) Then look at the **sample** answers on the next **three** pages, which **show** you how to answer the questions you'll get in this **unit**.

Dangerous Dogs

Dog attacks are becoming ever more common in the UK and something must be done to protect the public from this menace. Approximately 4,000 people were admitted to A&E departments last year after being bitten by a dog. This figure is unacceptable. The government needs to review and strengthen the current Dangerous Dogs Act, and bring in a licensing system to make sure only people who are fit to care for dogs are allowed to keep them.

1

Currently, UK law bans people from owning four different types of dog which are thought to be particularly dangerous. These dogs have been specifically bred for fighting and can be vicious when they are provoked. Anyone discovered to be keeping one of these dogs will be summoned to court and could face up to 6 months in prison and a £5000 fine, as well as having their dog put down. However, this is not deterring people from owning these types of dog — the number of dangerous dogs being kept as pets is increasing. West Midlands Police have reported that they seized twice as many dangerous dogs in 2009-10 than in 2008-9. While the current law is a step in the right direction, it needs to go much further. Banning dangerous types of dog is not the best solution to the problem of dog aggression.

2

Since banning dangerous types of dog has not worked, the government should reintroduce a dog licence, similar to the one that is needed in order to own a shotgun. Under the 1968 Firearms Act, anyone wishing to possess a shotgun must undergo background checks as well as having their house checked by a police officer to make sure it is suitable for weapons storage. In contrast, anyone who can afford to buy a dog is currently allowed to own one. Owners whose dogs have attacked people can be banned from owning a dog in the future, but by the time their dog has attacked someone, it's already too late.

3

The need for the homes of potential dog owners to be checked is even greater than the need to check the homes of people wishing to purchase a shotgun. Poor living conditions are a major factor in causing dogs to become aggressive. Dogs are active, social animals, and if they are left alone in cramped conditions, they often become bored and feel abandoned. This can lead them to attack other dogs and people.

4

In addition to potential dog owners having their homes checked, all dogs should have microchips inserted under their skin carrying their owner's contact details. This would force people to take more responsibility for the actions of their animal as it would allow police to track down the owners of any dangerous dogs.

5

It could be argued that this licensing proposal would be punishing responsible dog owners who are not putting the public in danger, but if these tougher rules prevent any more innocent children from being injured by dogs, surely it is worth the inconvenience to other people? We must prevent the tragedy of more people being attacked by dangerous dogs by introducing a dog licence.

6

Do Well in Unit Two — Section B

Some *Questions* will ask you to '*Explain* one *Strength* or *Weakness...*'

1) You might be asked to **explain** either a **strength** or a **weakness** of a piece of evidence used in a source document.
2) Read the question **carefully** to make sure you know **which** to write about.
3) Here's an **example** of a strength / weakness question and **how** to answer it.

1. In paragraph 1 of the source document, the author says that 'Approximately 4,000 people were admitted to A&E departments last year after being bitten by a dog.' Explain one **weakness** in the way this evidence is used.
[2 marks]

> The use of this evidence is weakened by the fact that it is out of context. The figure could be decreasing already, or it could have stayed the same, so it might not be as 'unacceptable' as the document suggests.

1. In paragraph 1 of the source document, the author says that 'Approximately 4,000 people were admitted to A&E departments last year after being bitten by a dog.' Explain one **strength** in the way this evidence is used.
[2 marks]

> This evidence is relevant to the conclusion that the problem of dangerous dogs should be addressed because it only refers to bites serious enough to need hospital treatment, not playful nips from family pets.

Some *Questions* will ask you to '*Give* an *Alternative Explanation...*'

1) Source documents often include **explanations** for **evidence** they've used.
2) You might be asked to think of an **alternative** explanation for the evidence in the **document**.
3) Here's an **example** of this type of question:

2. Paragraph 2 of the source document states that the increase in the number of dangerous dogs seized by West Midlands Police is a result of more people owning illegal dogs in the UK. Give an alternative explanation for this increase. [2 marks]

Remember — if you can think of an alternative explanation for evidence, this will weaken the conclusion. See p.43 for more.

4) According to the **examiner**, your answer's got to be '**clearly** expressed and **developed**' to get the full **two** marks. Here's an **example** of how you could answer this question:

> An alternative explanation for the increase in the number of dangerous dogs seized by West Midlands Police is that the police in this area spent more time and money on seizing dogs in 2009-10 than in 2008-9.

Franklin may have looked harmless, but his journalistic skills made him a very dangerous dog.

Some *Questions* will ask '*What* does the paragraph *Imply*?'

1) You **might** be asked to say what is being **implied** in a **paragraph** in the source document.
2) Your answer must follow **logically** from what's in the **paragraph**, and can't be something that's **already said** in the document.
3) Here's an **example** of this type of question and a possible **answer**.

Look back at p.36 for a definition of 'imply'.

3. What does the author imply in paragraph 5 of the source document? [2 marks]

> Paragraph 5 implies that many dog owners do not take responsibility for the actions of their dogs. ✓

This follows **logically** from paragraph 5 because if we **need** to '**force** people to take more responsibility' then many people must **not already** do this.

4) Be **careful** that your answer isn't too **strong**...

> Paragraph 5 implies that dog owners never take responsibility for the actions of their dogs. ✗

...or too **weak.**

> Paragraph 5 implies that a few dog owners do not take responsibility for the actions of their dogs. ✗

Do Well in Unit Two — Section B

Some *Questions* will ask you to 'Make *One* point of *Evaluation...*'

1) A **question** asking you to make '**one point** of evaluation' is just an '**evaluate**' question that only needs a **short** answer.

2) You'll need to make **one** point about how **well** a particular **element** of the argument works and **why**.

3) Here's an **example**:

> 4. In paragraph 3, the author draws an analogy between owning a dangerous dog and owning a shotgun. Make one point of evaluation about this analogy. [3 marks]

The two situations the author compares in this analogy are very different. Very few people want to own a shotgun so the police have enough time to carry out 'background checks' on every one of them. However, millions of people in the UK own dogs so it would not be practical to introduce a similar licence system as the police do not have the manpower to check millions of homes for 'poor living conditions.'

To get **all three** marks, you've got to:

1) make a '**relevant comparison**' between the two things in the **analogy**,

2) make a '**clear reference**' to the source document.

Sometimes '*Evaluate...*' questions are worth a lot of *Marks*

1) You might have to answer a **longer** question which asks you to **evaluate** more of the reasoning in the document.

2) These questions can be worth a **lot** of **marks** so jot down some ideas **before** you dive into writing your **answer**.

3) Here's an **example** of one of these questions:

> 5. Evaluate the reasoning in paragraphs 3 to 6 of the source document. In your answer you might consider:
> - flaws and appeals
> - the use of evidence
> - the use of analogies
> - other evaluation [9 marks]

For a question like this that's worth **9 marks**, you'll need to make **3 points**. There are **3 marks** available for each one. You need to:

1) Say **what** you're going to evaluate e.g. the argument commits the flaw of restricting the options.

2) **Refer** to the document in your answer e.g. say which two options the author gives.

3) Say **why** it's a strength/weakness e.g. there may be other possible options.

It's a good idea to briefly suggest an example of another possible option.

At the beginning of paragraph 3, the author's claim that since banning dangerous dogs has not worked, the only option is to reintroduce a licensing scheme commits the flaw of restricting the options. There might be other ways for the government to solve this problem that the author does not consider, such as compulsory dog-training classes.

Later on in paragraph 3, the author uses an analogy between owning a dangerous dog and owning a shotgun. Dogs and shotguns are both harmless if used carefully, but it is true that both are potentially dangerous so the analogy is strong enough to support the proposed introduction of a dog licence.

In paragraph 6, by saying that these rules could 'prevent any more innocent children from being injured by dogs', the author is using an appeal to emotion. It is extremely unlikely that these rules will prevent all future injuries so the appeal is inappropriate and does not support the conclusion.

The reasoning in paragraphs 3 to 6 only gives limited support to the conclusion that the UK government should reintroduce a dog licence scheme. The argument is weakened by the fact that, despite using a strong analogy, it presents the licence as the only possible option, and it uses an inappropriate appeal.

Sandra thought that drawing her analogy on the pavement might make it stronger.

Do Well in Unit Two — Section C

Here's a worked answer Supporting a Conclusion

6. Write an argument to **support** the following claim from paragraph 2:

    'Banning dangerous types of dog is not the best solution to the problem of dog aggression.'

    Marks are awarded for a developed and well-structured answer. It must include at least three reasons, an intermediate conclusion and a main conclusion, as well as examples and/or evidence. You may also include other argument elements.

    You can use ideas and information from the source document, but you must use them to construct a new argument. No marks will be awarded for the repetition of arguments from the source document.

> Make sure you don't reuse any of the reasons in the source.

> Starting with a counter-argument is a good way of introducing your conclusion.

> This intermediate conclusion follows from R1 & R2.

CA

R

IC

Many people argue that no one should be allowed to own types of dog that are dangerous because they might attack members of the public, injuring or even killing them. While it is true that dog attacks are a problem, banning specific types of dog is not the best way to solve it. Most so-called 'dangerous types of dog' never harm anyone and many experts argue that a dog's training is what makes it attack people. Therefore, it is unfair to ban entire types of dog just because a small number of badly trained dogs have attacked people in the past.

Supporters of the current law argue that a ban on dangerous dogs is necessary because aggressive types of dog are often used by criminals, such as gangs who use dogs as weapons to attack their enemies. However, if one type of dog is banned, then these gangs will simply train dogs of another type to be just as aggressive. In addition, many dog attacks involve a family pet and take place in the family home. This indicates that rather than banning particular types of dog, it would be better to educate parents about how their pets and children can mix safely. It is more important to inform people about dangers in life than it is to remove the danger altogether.

Therefore, banning dangerous types of dog is not the best solution to the problem of dog aggression.

> It's a good idea to state your conclusion at the beginning of your argument — it makes it more focused.

> R1 & R2

> It's often easier to think up examples rather than evidence using your general knowledge.

> Hypothetical reasoning which dismisses the CA.

> Remember to finish with your main conclusion.

Here are some Ideas for Challenging the same Conclusion

Banning dangerous dogs is the best solution to the problem of dog aggression because:

* More and more **criminal gangs** are using dangerous dogs as **weapons**.
* **Banning** them would **stop** people seeing them as a **fashion accessory**.
* **Other** things that are **dangerous** to society are banned **already**, e.g. drugs.
* **Most** attacks are by a **few types** of dog (although there are **exceptions**).

> See p.60 for more on how to write a conclusion to challenge a claim.

All good thinks must come to an end...

It's hard to believe how far we've come in only a few sections. Just think, not long ago, you didn't know the difference between a main conclusion and an intermediate conclusion... (If you've forgotten, you'd better flip this book back to the beginning and have another look.) You deserve a big pat on the back and maybe a little something to say well done. (Now where did I put the biscuits...)

Glossary

ability to see or perceive How well someone was able to witness an event, or how much access they have to all the facts of an argument. One of the credibility criteria.

ad hominem When an argument tries to get you to dismiss a counter-argument or accept a conclusion based on the good or bad qualities of the person arguing, rather than their argument.

ambiguous A statement or word is ambiguous if it can mean more than one thing, and it's not clear which is meant or intended.

analogy A comparison that tries to persuade you that if you accept a claim about one of the things being compared, you must also accept the same claim about the other thing being compared.

appeal Part of an argument that tries to persuade you that a conclusion is true without using rational reasons.

appeal to authority Part of an argument that refers to the opinion of an expert or someone in charge to justify a conclusion.

appeal to emotion Part of an argument that tries to persuade you that a conclusion is true by making you feel a certain way.

appeal to history Part of an argument which tries to convince you that because something's happened a certain way in the past, it'll also happen that way in the future.

appeal to popularity Part of an argument that tries to persuade you that a conclusion is true because lots of people believe that it is.

appeal to tradition Part of an argument that tries to persuade you that just because something's been done a certain way in the past, that's the way it should be done now.

arguing from one thing to another When an argument's reasons and conclusion are about different things. This is also called an unrelated conclusion.

argument A speech or piece of writing that tries to convince you to accept a conclusion. An argument must have at least one reason, and only one main conclusion.

argument element Part of an argument — e.g. the reasons, evidence and conclusion are all argument elements.

argument indicator A word that shows that a reason or conclusion might be coming up — e.g. therefore, because.

assertion A conclusion that isn't supported by any reasons.

assess When you assess something, you have to discuss one side, discuss the other side and then draw a conclusion — e.g. if a question asks you to assess a document's credibility you've got to say what increases its credibility, what decreases it, and then say how credible you think it is overall.

assumption An unstated reason that is needed for the argument to work.

begging the question If an argument is begging the question you have to accept the conclusion before you can accept the reasons.

belief Something someone thinks is true.

bias An irrational preference for a particular side of an argument. One of the credibility criteria.

circular argument An argument where the conclusion repeats one of the reasons.

challenge A question that highlights a possible weakness in an argument

claim A statement that it's possible to question or disagree with.

coherent A coherent argument makes sense — it's consistent and is not illogical or confusing.

common notation Using letters to stand for the different elements of an argument so you can see its structure more clearly — e.g. R = Reason, C = Conclusion.

conclusion The suggestion, idea, belief or theory that the argument is trying to persuade you to accept. The conclusion is often referred to as the main conclusion.

conflation A type of flaw where two words or concepts are used as if they mean the same thing when they actually have different meanings.

conflict Two sources or claims that disagree with each other are conflicting. Conflicting sources or claims are also called inconsistent sources or claims.

confusing cause and effect When an argument reverses a cause and its effects, saying that the effect brought about the cause.

Glossary

confusing necessary and sufficient conditions When an argument treats sufficient conditions as necessary, or necessary conditions as sufficient.

consistent / consistency Accounts are consistent if it is possible for all their claims to be true at the same time. Consistency is one of the credibility criteria.

contradict Statements contradict each other if they say exactly opposite things — e.g. one witness says the getaway car was blue and another says it was pink.

converse A statement that reverses the two events in a statement of hypothetical reasoning — e.g. the converse of "If it is a square then it has four sides," is "If it has four sides then it is a square."

corroboration When two sources or claims agree with each other. One of the credibility criteria.

counter Countering an argument means disagreeing with it by providing a claim or argument that goes against it.

counter-argument Part of an argument that disagrees with the main conclusion.
Counter-arguments always have a conclusion and at least one reason.

counter-assertion A statement that goes against the conclusion of an argument.
Counter-assertions are not supported by any reasons.

CRAVEN A handy way of remembering the credibility criteria: corroboration / consistency, reputation, ability to see or perceive, vested interest / bias, experience / expertise, neutrality.

credibility How believable someone or something is.

credibility criteria Tools that can be used to help judge the credibility of a document, person or organisation.

evaluate If you're asked to evaluate something, you need to look at its strengths and weaknesses and decide how effective it is overall.

evidence Information that is used to support reasons — e.g. facts, figures, quotes or personal observations.

example A description of a real situation that illustrates a reason.

experience Someone has experience if they've done or witnessed something that most other people haven't. One of the credibility criteria.

expertise Someone has expertise if they have specialist skills or training which give them knowledge other people don't have. One of the credibility criteria.

explanation A way of trying to improve our understanding of something by describing why it is the way it is.

false cause When an argument claims that event A caused event B, but actually event A just happened before event B. Also known as post hoc.

false dichotomy When an argument tries to present its conclusion as the best option by only discussing a limited range of choices. This is also known as restricting the options.

flaw A mistake in the reasoning used to link an argument's reasons to its conclusion. Flaws always weaken arguments.

general principle A general rule about how we should behave which can apply to many different situations.

hasty generalisation When an argument uses a claim about a few things to support a conclusion about lots of things, or everything.

hypothetical reasoning A claim saying that if one thing happens, then something else will happen as a result of it.

imply If an unstated claim logically follows from the meaning of a statement, then the statement implies that claim — e.g. "The woman was murdered" implies that she is dead.

inconsistent An argument is inconsistent if it contains two statements that can't both be true at the same time.

infer To look at reasons or evidence and decide what conclusions they could support.

intermediate conclusion A conclusion made on the way to the main conclusion. It's supported by reasons, but it also acts as a reason for supporting the main conclusion.

knowledge Being certain that something's true because you have information to prove it.

necessary A necessary condition for something is one that must happen or be true for something else to happen — e.g. to be a bachelor it is necessary to be male.

neutral Being neutral means not having any bias or vested interest. One of the credibility criteria.

Glossary

opinion A personal belief based on taste or preference, not on facts.

Opposite Test A test used to work out whether an assumption is necessary to make an argument work.

plausibility How reasonable a claim is, or how likely an outcome is.

post hoc When an argument claims that event A caused event B, but actually event A just happened before event B. Also known as false cause.

primary evidence First-hand evidence which comes directly from an eyewitness.

reason Part of an argument that aims to persuade you that the conclusion is true. An argument must have at least one reason, but most have more.

reasonableness Another word for plausibility.

reasoning The process of drawing a conclusion from reasons and evidence.

reasoning from wrong actions A name for the 'tu quoque' and 'two wrongs don't make a right' flaws.

refute Refuting a claim means giving reasons to prove that it's wrong.

reliability A source or document is reliable if it can be trusted.

repudiate Repudiating a claim means saying that it's wrong without giving any reasons why.

reputation The opinion people have of someone. One of the credibility criteria.

restricting the options When an argument tries to present its conclusion as the best option by only discussing a limited range of choices. This is also known as a false dichotomy.

secondary evidence Second-hand evidence which comes through another person — it is indirect.

simplifying causal relations When an argument claims that one thing was entirely responsible for making something happen, when actually it happened because of several factors.

slippery slope A flaw which says that a small event will cause an extreme result, but gives us no reason to accept that the event and the result are properly linked.

straw person / straw man When an argument misrepresents or distorts a counter-argument to make it easier to dismiss.

strengths Parts of an argument that help support the conclusion effectively.

structure The different parts of an argument and the logical way they're linked together.

sufficient A sufficient condition for something is one that is enough for that something to happen — e.g. eating a full English breakfast is sufficient to stop you feeling hungry.

support Supporting something means backing it up by giving reasons to accept it.

sweeping generalisation When an argument uses a claim about many things to support a conclusion about one individual case.

Therefore Test The test used to check which part of an argument is the conclusion, and which parts are the reasons. It can also be used to distinguish between intermediate and main conclusions.

tu quoque When an argument defends an action by saying that the same action has also been done by other people — e.g. it's ok to drive faster than the speed limit because everyone else does.

two wrongs don't make a right When an argument justifies a harmful action by saying that other people have behaved badly in a different way — e.g. I beat him up because he insulted my family.

unrelated conclusion When an argument's reasons and conclusion are about different things. This is also called arguing from one thing to another.

vested interest Someone has vested interest if they will gain something from supporting a particular side of an argument, or lose something if they don't. One of the credibility criteria.

weaknesses Parts of an argument that don't support the conclusion.

Index

OO573896